A Taste of
CIDER

Harvesting the crop

A *Taste of*
CIDER

SHIRLEY HARRISON .

Illustrations by Graeme Jenner

DAVID & CHARLES
Newton Abbot London North Pomfret (Vt)

Metric equivalents have not been given for spoon measures; these are usually taken to be 5ml for a teaspoon, 10ml for a desertspoon and 15ml for a tablespoon. Similarly, a cup measure, where used, is normally taken as equivalent to 6fl oz or 125g (dry weight).

British Library Cataloguing in Publication Data

Harrison, Shirley
A taste of cider.
1. Cookery (Cider)
I. Title
641.6'2   TX726
ISBN 0–71538216–0

Phototypeset by Keyspools Ltd, Golborne, Lancs
and printed in Great Britain
by Redwood Burn Limited, Trowbridge
for David & Charles (Publishers) Limited
Brunel House Newton Abbot Devon

Published in the United States of America
by David & Charles Inc
North Pomfret Vermont 05053 USA

To Philip Evemy, friend and colleague, whose professional enthusiasm first gave me a taste for cider.

ACKNOWLEDGEMENTS

So many people have shared their knowledge with me; my thanks especially to Professor Walter Minchinton at Exeter University, Fred Roach BSc, OBE, cider sage and former adviser to ADAS, and Stanley and Margaret Baldock of Sussex whose countrywide researches have been the love of a lifetime.

CONTENTS

The Summer oversped, October drawing on sir,
The apples good and red glowing in the sun sir,
As the season does advance, your apples for to gather,
I bid you catch the chance to pick them in fair weather.

When to the pommy ground, you squeeze out all the juice sir,
Thus fill a cask well bound and set it by for use sir,
Oh bid the cider flow in ploughing or in sowing,
The healthiest drink I know in reaping or in mowing.

INTRODUCTION

The taste of cider is a liquid evocation of the English countryside; of hedgerow walks, pub benches in the sun, the smell of stubble on an autumn day; being young and happy and broke.

The story of cider has been woven into the life and folklore of rural England for at least 1,000 years. As a drink it has been a national favourite here longer than in almost any other country: for centuries farmers made it, housewives cooked with it and doctors extolled its medicinal magic. Yet it is really only since the last war that cider has become a high flyer in the kitchen.

Today its production is a matter of national pride. It has found its way into the picnic fare of Henley, Glyndebourne and Ascot; has been blessed by inclusion in WI cookbooks to be poured into the best of British scones, Christmas pudding and eel pies and is exported to over 100 countries.

Gone are the hazy days when cider-was-scrumpy, and that was that; when half a pint would buckle your legs or blow the top off your head. Though an increasing number of farmers are now nostalgically (and astutely) restoring their presses and reviving the powerful, old-fashioned stuff in flagons for tourists and holiday-makers, 98 per cent is factory-made, mostly now by four main producers. In Hereford there is Bulmers, in Somerset there is Taunton, in Somerset and Norfolk, Coates Gaymers and in Sussex, Merrydown.

Working to a formula and a formidable list of twenty-one permitted practices laid down by the nineteen members of the National Association of Cidermakers, they turn out dozens of different brands, each with a distinctive flavour and kick of its own wherever you buy it. A far cry from the hit and miss methods of history. For although the origins of cider are humble, new techniques make it possible to produce a drink comparable with many wines for drinking and, increasingly, cooking.

The recipes I have chosen are a personal 'anthology' using the best-known, nationally available supermarket brands and gathered not only from the cidermarkets themselves but from people or places whose names are linked with the history of cider and the English countryside.

There is no cachet to cider-making. There is no such thing as a cider snob, cider has little of the mystique of the world's great wines, and there's no need to feel knowledgeable to enjoy it! Yet there are marked variations in taste and strength which are worth understanding.

So, what exactly is this drink which visitors from abroad have come to regard as one of the traditional tastes of England?

British cider is made from apple juice, specially cultivated yeast and varying amounts of sugar and water. We drink approximately 50 million gallons of it a year.

36% of all adults drink cider
Men   54% of all cider drinkers
Women   46% of all cider drinkers

Age	18–24	28%
	25–34	23%
	35–44	16%
	45–54	14%
	55–64	10%
	65 and over	9%

AB (middle/upper middle class)	21%
C1 (lower middle class)	23%
C2 (skilled working class)	33%
DE (lower working class)	23%

(*British Market Research Bureau Target Group Index 1979*)

THE APPLE

The apple is one of the oldest cultivated fruits in the world – known in Babylon and Ancient Egypt and cared for later by Pomona the Roman goddess of garden fruits (whose name is recalled today in the French for apple – pomme, and in Pomagne).

Modern apple growing, a mechanised and highly intensified

industry, is watched over by such prestigious organisations as The Long Ashton Research Centre at Bristol, the East Malling Research Station in Kent (where they think up many of the new fruit names) and the Royal Horticultural Society Garden at Wisley, where they grow such historic varieties as Sir Isaac Newton's Flower of Kent.

These days an orchard is a factory and many growers have replaced our familiar, old-fashioned, picture-postcard trees with much smaller bush varieties which offer a greater return for money. Growing to only eight feet (2.4m) they are easier to harvest and crop after three years instead of fifteen. So, the sight of sheep grazing beneath the spring blossom of gnarled old trees is vanishing; in place of family teams up ladders at harvest time are mechanical shakers, blowers and gatherers often manned by students on vacation.

There are two distinct schools of thought about the type of fruit best used for cidermaking: that of the West Country – and the rest. Traditionally West Country cider has always been made from purpose-grown fruit (because, say 'the rest', the soil there isn't good enough for anything better). In Kent and Sussex they claim that cider made from their dessert and cooking apples, from the 'finest orchards in the world', must be a finer drink (only, say the West Country growers, because Garden of England soil *can't* produce proper cider fruit)! The results are certainly different. Your choice depends entirely on your taste buds.

There are four main categories of cider apple.

Sweets (Court Royal, Sweet Alford, Sweet Coppin). These are low in acid and tannin and, being the most bland, are used to soften ciders made with stronger fruit.

Sharps (Crimson King and Brown's Apple) and

Bittersharp (Stoke Red, Foxwhelp, Kingston Black, Bramley and Cox). These two categories are fairly high in both acid and tannin. Most dessert and culinary apples fall in this category.

Bittersweet (Dabinette Yarlington Mill, Tremlett's Bitter). These are low in acid and high in tannin which is responsible for two sensations on the palate – astringency and bitterness. Bitter-sweets, therefore, have a range of combinations of these two which impart the characteristic flavour of English cider.

11

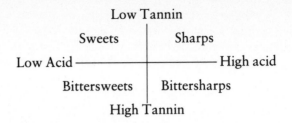

By comparison dessert and cooking apples, such as Bramley, Cox, Grenadiers or James Grieve, have a lower sugar content, less malic acid and no tartaric acid.

I

CIDER FOR ALL SEASONS

Cider of sorts was probably always made wherever the apple grew naturally, and the two stories are necessarily intertwined. It would be tempting to imagine that Adam and Eve enjoyed its taste in the Garden of Eden at the beginning of time. But strangely the Bible never once names the forbidden fruit which caused the downfall of Man.

Could this be an idea which developed because of a mistranslation of centuries ago? It is more likely that the fruit Eve offered Adam from the Tree of Knowledge was originally the indigenous pomegranate (the apple full of grain) – and you can't make cider from a pomegranate! Even so, how odd it is that the Turkish for pomegranate was *side*, pronounced 'seeder', although most historians – who ought to know – claim that cider originates from the Hebrew word for strong drink, *cekar*.

In Britain we know, from remains found at Windmill Hill in Somerset, that Bronze Age Britons were eating the indigenous crab apple. So it seems probable they had discovered its properties as a drink. Verjuice, as it was later called, was really the direct ancestor of cider. For centuries it was used in cooking whenever today we would use a sharp cider or even lemon juice. One medieval recipe suggests:

> Gather crabbes as soon as the kernels turn blacke and lay they in a heap to sweat and take them into troughs and crush with beetles. Make a bagge of coarse hair cloth and fill it with crabbes and presse and run the liquor into hogsheads.

Crab Apple Jelly
A colourful and fruity jelly to eat with meat, or bread and butter for tea. Makes about 3lb and will keep for a good twelve months.

6lb (2.7kg) crab apples (red and green variety are best)
3pt (1.7L) Woodpecker cider

1lb (450g) granulated sugar to every 1pt (550ml) juice
2–3 strips lemon rind

Wash the apples, wipe and cut in half. Put fruit into a large pan with the cider and simmer until very soft, stirring and crushing occasionally. Turn the pulp into a clean, dry cloth or jelly bag to drip, and leave overnight. Measure the juice and add the sugar in proportion. Return to the pan and stir over heat until the sugar has completely dissolved. Add lemon rind and boil rapidly until jelly will set. This is when a sugar thermometer measures 107°C or 220°F, or when a dsp of jelly crinkles up and feels tacky when placed on a cold saucer. Remove lemon rind, pour into dry, warm, sterile jars. Cover with wax discs and tops.

There is no record that the Romans drank cider, which is strange because they were the first to develop orchards and understand grafting. After the Romans left, none of the tribes who settled in Britain mention its use. The Anglo Saxons cultivated Appel tuns (orchards) but we don't know that they drank the by-product.

The Benedictine monks at Battle Abbey

14

Cider production really properly began – like so many other enthusiasms – with the Normans. The Northern French were already great cider drinkers before the Conquest – between 742 and 748 Charlemagne had a cidermaker travelling with him. It is known too that William The Conqueror's men boosted their sagging morale during the long, boring wait for the winds to set fair for England on extra rations of wine and cider!

Battle Abbey, dedicated in 1094, was to become one of the most important Norman abbeys, situated as it was on the main route from London to the sea, and the people of Battle village today claim that here indeed was 'the birthplace of the nation'. Certainly the south east was the birthplace of commercial cidermaking and there in the Battle Abbey cellars the Benedictine monks produced cider for their own, and for external, consumption. In 1275 the cellarers' rolls recall 'Brother N Cellarer of Battle from May 3rd to the 3rd year of the reign of King Edward I to the day after Michaelmas next, following in the same year received 24s for 2 casks (tonnells) of cider sold.'

There are no longer any monks at Battle Abbey – the nearest Benedictine house is Worth Abbey, near Crawley, Sussex – and this recipe from the Worth Abbey kitchens is based on one of the oldest of all formulae.

Bacon cooked with Dried Peas or Beans   *serves 6*

2–2½lb (900g–1.13kg) hock or shoulder of gammon
¼lb (225g) split peas, lentils or chick peas
1 small onion
2 tbsp chopped celery
1½oz (35–40g) butter

1½oz (35–40g) plain flour
½pt (275ml) dry cider
2oz (50g) stoneless raisins
¼pt (150ml) gammon stock
2 tsp demerara sugar
2 tbsp chopped parsley

Wash the gammon and place in large bowl with pulses, cover with cold water and leave overnight or for 8 hours. Drain. Put meat and pulses in large, heavy-based pan, and cover with fresh cold water. Bring to the boil, lower heat and cover pan with lid. Simmer for 1½ hours or till hock is tender. Lift meat from pan and leave aside to cool slightly. Leave pulses to cook for further 30 minutes. Skin hock while still warm and cut meat into 1in (2.5cm) cubes, discarding fat.

Peel and finely chop onion and prepare celery. Melt butter in

15

heavy-based pan and fry onions and celery gently till soft. Remove pan from heat and stir in flour till butter is absorbed. Gradually stir in cider to make a smooth sauce. Return pan to heat and bring to simmering, stirring continuously. Mix in raisins and enough gammon stock to make a creamy sauce. Blend in sugar and continue cooking for further 10 minutes on low heat. Add cubed hock to sauce and heat through thoroughly.

Drain the pulses and toss in a little butter and parsley. Spoon meat and sauce into centre of a warmed serving dish and surround with the pulses.

Pears in Dry Cider   *serves 4*
From Mrs Pamela Clovier, Battle housewife.

1–2lb (450–900g) Conference pears (small misshapen fruit is fine)

cinnamon or grated nutmeg
dry cider

demerara or soft brown sugar

Peel, core and thinly slice the pears and place in layers in a fireproof dish. Sprinkle each layer with sugar, cinnamon or nutmeg to the top of the dish finishing with sugar and cinnamon layer. Pour over enough dry cider to nearly cover; place lid or foil over dish and cook slowly for 2 hours at 150°C (300°F) Mark 2.

Throughout the Middle Ages farming became more settled. Taxes were extracted from the owners of orchards – so the great religious houses craftily cultivated 'gardens', where they developed a more scientific approach to fruit growing.

The first recorded cooking apple was sold in Oxford in 1296 – it was a Costard, hence the word 'costermonger', or seller of costards. The earliest known eating apple was the Permain, noted in 1205.

With the spread of small orchards, national consumption increased and eventually most communities had a small cider mill to meet their own needs. Even so, in 1272 cider production in Sussex wasn't meeting local demand and the Winchelsea Custom Rolls mention considerable imports from France. In 1275 a Richard de Clifford was accused of stealing a press and mill from the widow of Geoffrey de Bosco of Pagham, Sussex. By 1330 ordinary people everywhere made cider and labourers were sometimes paid partially in kind. One monastic gardener was given 'the crop from one apple tree, and two gallons of cider daily'.

The Church even forbade the practice of baptising babies in it – presumably cider was believed to be safer than polluted water! They then decided to stake a claim in this growing business and in 1341 the Nonae Rolls recorded parishes nationwide paying considerable cider tithes.

During the Hundred Years' War from 1337 to 1453 the French banned exports of wine, which meant that the aristocracy had to develop a liking for home-produced cider, although it was even then a working man's drink.

Could it be that the scholar William Wycliffe himself had had a drop too much when translating his Bible? According to him the Angel says to Zacharias in *Luke* (Ch. 1, v 15), 'He shall not drink wyn and syder.' Had he, too, wrongly translated the Hebrew word for strong drink?

The Black Death of 1348–9 killed off one third of the population and heralded a period of depression and unrest which lasted through to Tudor times. Until the reign of Henry VIII varieties of home-grown fruits and vegetables were very limited and there was little interest in horticulture. Gradually, as monastic influence declined and Henry eventually dissolved the monasteries, power switched to the new landed gentry. The stately-home owners loved gardening, and many of them took an active interest in fruit growing. One of these was Richard Harris, fruiterer to King Henry VIII. He decided to improve the state of British horticulture. 'The plants our ancestors had brought out of Normandy had lost their native verdour' he complained. He imported grafts from France and the Low Countries and in 1553 he planted an orchard at Newgardens, Teynham, Kent.

If Battle saw the birth of a nation then Teynham surely saw the flowering of the Garden of England. It was a momentous step in the history of horticulture and, consequently, cidermaking. Writing in his *Perambulation of England* (1570) Lambarde described how 'this is the cherrie garden and apple orchard of Kent, the parent of all the rest from whom they have drawn the good juice of all their pleasant fruit'. Today the orchards of Tony Norris on the Honeyball Estate at Teynham form part of that original plantation, from which he still supplies local cider-makers with fruit.

In the ironically up-to-date preface of a book called *Fruiterers' Secrets*, published at the turn of the sixteenth century, the first exports of fruit are recorded with some delight.

Teynham is the chief mother of all other orchards. Although there were some stores of fruit in England yet there were both rare fruits and fine lasting fruit. Thanks to God divers gentlemen and others taking a delight in grafting have planted many orchards and by reason of the increase that is now growing in diverse parts of this land of such fine fruit there is no need of any foreign fruit but we are able to serve other places.

All through the sixteenth century advances in fruit growing were helped by the prolific publication of specialist books on cookery and on fruit growing. Here are four recipes, sixteenth century in flavour, modern in method.

Cider Syllabub   serves 4

In Elizabethan times the cow was milked direct into a bucket containing cider or wine and the frothy mixture then sweetened and served immediately. It was sometimes known as Hatted Kit. Syllabub today is rich and creamy.

juice and rind of ½ lemon	2oz (50g) caster sugar
¼pt (150ml) sweet cider	¾pt (425ml) double cream
1 tbsp brandy	

Finely grate lemon rind and squeeze out the juice. Put rind and juice in a bowl with the cider, brandy and sugar and stir until sugar is dissolved. Pour in the cream and whisk until peaks appear. Spoon into individual glasses and serve with langue-de-chats, wafer biscuits or brandy snaps.

Posset   serves 4

1½lb (675g) cooking apples	1 rounded tbsp cornflour
½pt (275ml) sweet cider	whipped cream
sugar to sweeten	browned almonds
¼ tsp cinnamon	

Peel, core and roughly slice apples. Place in pan with the cider, sugar and cinnamon, cover, and cook gently till soft. Sieve or blend to a purée. Mix cornflour to a smooth paste with a little

18

extra cider, add the apple purée and bring to boil slowly. Simmer for 2 minutes. Remove from heat and leave to cool slightly before turning into glass dishes to serve. Decorate with almonds and cream.

Venison soaked in Cider
There is a revived taste for venison today and a growing number of deer farms supply meat at prices comparable with beef.

Cut the venison into strips and marinate in cider. Drain, dust with pepper and flour, and fry. Then lay in a braising dish with allspice and a dash of cider, vinegar, some bay leaves and cloves. Add just enough water to moisten and cook slowly for hours. Towards end add mushrooms in layers over the top and serve with green vegetables, flat crisp fried potatoes and watercress.

Old Fashioned Ham
For centuries the pig was the most important domestic creature. Its production and annual slaughter was accompanied by all kinds of rural ritual, and absolutely no part was ever wasted. As the killing coincided roughly with cidermaking, it is natural that the use of cider with pork should have been appreciated by country cooks from all ages. Even today pork is the meat we think of first when cooking with cider. This is a recipe which, with slight variations, could be 400 years old.

Soak a ham for 24 hours, changing the water frequently. Make a bed of vegetables and their peelings at the bottom of a heavy pan. Use onions (including the golden outer skin), celery roots and leaves, tops of parsnips, the outer skin of turnips and a sprinkling of herbs and peppercorns. Place the ham on the vegetables with 1pt (550ml) sour cider (dry will do), 8oz (225g) sugar, 1lb (450g) black treacle, and cover with apple peelings. Cover everything with water and simmer for 4 hours. Allow to cool leaving the ham in the liquid. Next day drain the ham, remove the rind, glaze with brown sugar and cloves and finish in the oven (this would once have been done in front of an open fire). Decorate with a ham frill.

19

The Earl of Scudamore

In the seventeenth century, the climate, excellent soil and easy transportation meant that the Garden of England fruit found its way mostly to London. Apples in Somerset and Hereford had no such outlet. Roads were bad and there were few canals. Farmers there specialised in trees that were grown in huge quantities specifically for cidermaking – and so began the growth of the traditional West Country cider industry.

Young Lord Scudamore tired of life at the court of Charles I and retired to Holme Lacy, Hereford, to indulge his interest in horticulture. His enthusiasm resulted in the development of the famous Redstreak apple which was to mark the next major stage in the development of cidermaking. And indeed, in 1656, Dr John Beale recorded King Charles's preference for cider to wine!

Throughout the rest of Britain cider production remained mainly in the hands of the farmer's wife. The better the stuff she produced, the better the quality of labourer who applied for work. For employers usually made up the wages of their workers with cider, a practice known as 'truck' which was finally forbidden in 1877. It was a poor quality stuff made from the second pressings and was called Ciderkin or Purr. Three pints a day was the usual ration, upped to four during haymaking.

Individual efforts were made to improve the taste, but there was no control over fermentation so that huge amounts of unpredictable and sometimes lethal stuff were produced. Sometimes steak, fat bacon or rabbit skins would be added to give vitamins and nutrients. Raisins, wheat and barley produced extra alcohol during fermentation, and beetroot and burnt sugar were used for colouring. In Cornwall miners ran sheep's blood into the cask in which aromatic gums were often burnt, and the cider was poured in while the cask was still full of smoke.

In Wales they believed duck-pond water added a little extra something – but that one farm's water added to the cider of another would be disastrous!

If a higher quality of cider was needed for social drinking, rather than as a perk for the ploughman, then the cider was left in open-topped vats for a few days before it was syphoned into a cask with a bag of mixed herbs. The yeast was starved of food this way and the cider was left naturally sweet. This method was used into the twentieth century and called 'keeving'.

The seventeenth century also saw improvements in cider-making equipment. Traditionally apples were left on the ground to rot and 'bring out their crude phlegmatic humour'. The farmer's wife would then pound them herself on the kitchen table, or in a hollowed tree trunk in the yard. Better still was the horse mill. These horse-drawn stone mills were introduced over 400 years ago and some can still be found, especially in the West Midlands. Mostly, they were made in apple-growing areas near to a supply of acid-resistant stone, such as the granite areas of Devon and Cornwall. Fifty to seventy turns of the millstone crushed 150–225kg of apples. Two or three men could make 100 gallons a day.

In 1678 John Worlidge of Petersfield, Hampshire, produced the first-ever book on cider, *The Vinetum Britannicum*, which listed some of the best cider varieties available – Slack ma Girdle ('a great bearer', good for the kitchen) and Go-no-further-with-Red-Side! But even more important he invented some of the first mechanical presses and mills to make production easier.

His 'Ingenio' was the grand-daddy of them all. A modified version on wheels called a 'scratter' was later used by the

The horse-drawn mill

travelling cidermaker on his autumnal visits around the countryside (and even today the rotary press sold to home cidermakers in most wineshops is little different from Worlidge's original). Later, by the mid-eighteenth century, screw presses had also become popular, which were first made of wood and then of iron.

In 1684 Richard Haines of Sullington in Sussex took out the first patent for a drink he called Cider Royal, which was a blend of pure and distilled apple juice. He described his process thus:

> An art or method of preparing, improving and meliorating cyder, perry and the juice of liqors of wilding crabbs so as to put the strength or goodness of two or three hogsheads into one and render the same much more wholesome and delightful.
>
> Put one hogshead of cyder into a copper still and then put the same into your other hogshead and fill it up, stir it about well and keep it close stopt except one day in ten or twenty let it lie open five or six hours. Within three months this will be as strong as the best French wines and as pleasing – though different in taste.

In times of national poverty or of cidermakers' affluence, the Government has raised revenue by taxes on the drink. This was done after the Civil War, and again to help pay for the Seven Years' War in 1763 – with astonishingly dramatic results. Excisemen raided people's homes looking for presses, and in Parliament William Pitt opposed the bill with the immortal words 'an Englishman's home is his castle'. At Ledbury in Gloucestershire in 1763 the local paper reported:

> A procession was made through the principal parts of this town by servants of the cidermerchants ... the day the Cyder Act took place ... in the following manner viz a man with a drum covered with black crepe beating the dead march, drumsticks reverted, two mutes with crepe hat hands and black cloaks and empty barrels upon a bier carried by six poor farmers dressed in cyder hair clothes; the bells rung muffled all day and every face expressed a sympathetic sorrow for the impending ruin that waits the country.

23

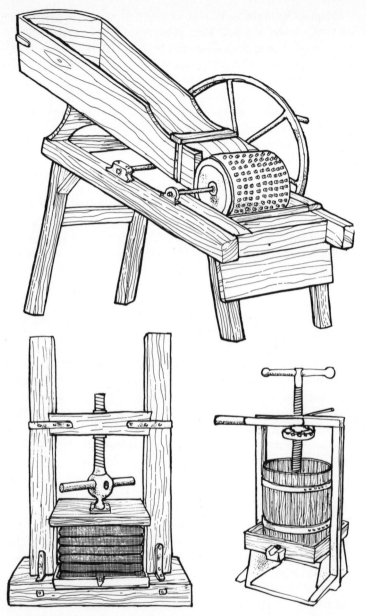

(*Top*) An eighteenth-century mill or 'scratter'. (*Bottom left*) An eighteenth-century screw press. (*Bottom right*) A modern press, available either in wine shops or you can 'do-it-yourself'

During the eighteenth and nineteenth centuries surplus cider led to the birth of a new kind of merchant, that of the ciderman. These were the middle men who in one year bought as much as 600,000 gallons in Hereford (one third of the total production) and sold it to France or Germany. There it was often mixed with cheap wine and returned to Britain as port or sherry!

As the population increased, the need was for more beef and grain, which meant that at the turn of the century cider orchards gradually were neglected and the farmer had no incentive to replant. Cider was still the farmworkers' favourite – but the quality was poor. As Victorian morality got the upper hand, temperance men went to work. Farmers were encouraged to pay their men in cash not kind, often called Dry Cider.

Even so, a few far-sighted men worked to improve the state of the orchards and the efficiency of machinery, and eventually the great flush of scientific and industrial knowledge which swept the country during the nineteenth century had its effect on the cider business, and helped pave the way for twentieth-century mass production.

The principles of cidermaking today are almost exactly the same as they were 1,000 years ago – just that the machinery is bigger and better! Instead of a hollow tree trunk and cheese on a wooden press it is now possible to install a $£\frac{1}{4}$ million machine and press 1,400 gallons an hour from 8 tons of fruit. Each manufacturer may have a slight variation on the theme.

Longest established of today's 'big four' producers is the Norfolk-based family of Gaymer. Farmer Robert Gaymer made cider in the village of Banham in the eighteenth century, but his great grandson, William, developed the small-scale cottage craft into a fully fledged commercial enterprise in 1870. He died in 1937 at the age of ninety-four leaving a thriving business for his son William, and grandson, also William. In 1968 Gaymers merged with the newer Somerset company of Coates.

The second to be founded was Bulmers. In 1887, on the advice of his mother, Henry Bulmer, younger son of the Rector of Credenhill in Hereford, started pressing apples from his father's orchards. Henry was twenty at the time, and Mrs Bulmer advised him wisely – 'food and drink never go out of fashion'. In 1888 he made 4,000 gallons of cider, and today Bulmers are the world's largest manufacturers, turning out around 25 million gallons a year.

The travelling cidermaker

What was the magic formula? It was Henry Bulmer's final isolation of the wild yeast which had hitherto dominated fermentation and made cidermaking unpredictable and the tastes variable. Together with other cider enthusiasts, and backed by the Amateur Woolhope Club of Hereford, he conducted experiments based on the work of Louis Pasteur. His results made it possible for taste and quality to be controlled so that at last, with modern bottling and speedy transport, the public knew that cider bought in Scotland would be exactly the same as cider in Somerset.

Together with his friends Mr R. Neville Grenville, of Butleigh in Somerset and scientific pioneer in cidermaking, and Mr C. W. Radcliffe Cooke, MP for Much Marcle in Hereford (known as MP for cider), he promoted the product with great enthusiasm. In 1903 they founded the National Fruit and Cider Institute at Long Ashton which eventually joined forces with today's respected Long Ashton Research Centre, as part of the University of Bristol.

Cider had 'arrived' socially. And in 1911 Bulmers were the first cidermakers appointed to hold a Royal Warrant.

The third company to succeed commercially was the one which became the Taunton Cider Company. Yet another reverend gentleman, seeing the popularity of cider, began making it at the turn of the century from his rectory at Heathfield near Taunton. He was the Rev. Thomas Cornish, and so popular was his brew that word reached the Royal ears and he began to supply Queen Victoria. Together with his gardener, Arthur Moor, and friend George Pallet, he opened a cider mill at Norton Fitzwarren in Somerset, but it was not until 1921 that the name 'Taunton Cider Company' was registered. At that time Taunton had 6 employees producing 10,000 gallons, compared with 430 people producing several million gallons today.

As roads and canals improved, distribution became easier and of course advertising became more sophisticated. But two world wars took a toll of the cider business and it was not until the spread of commercial television in the 1960s that the cider market was stimulated into growth once more.

The fourth large cidermaking enterprise began in a small way when, just after demob in 1946, two young men renewed a pre-war hobby and began making cider in the garage of a house called Merrydown in Sussex. They had a hunch that it might be possible to make a good cider from dessert and cooking apples from the Garden of England's 'finest orchards in the world'. The hunch paid off. Jack Ward and Ian Howie succeeded in producing a cider of wine-like character – 18 per cent proof no less. They called it Vintage Cider, and it rapidly gained the reputation amongst young people as a leg buckler.

The Merrydown Vintage Cider of those heady days took a knock when the Chancellor, Harold Macmillan, slapped a 10s 6d tax on all ciders and perries over 15 per cent proof. Undeterred, Jack Ward and Ian Howie upped their strength to 22 per cent proof and pressed on. Increasing duty in the 1960s and 1970s turned the wheel full circle and in 1975 the company introduced a new, slightly sparkling vintage cider at 14 per cent proof. It was this that took them from the garage to number 4 in the cider league.

Of course there have been other names which conjure up the memory of many a happy session at the local pub – Whiteways, for instance, who merged with Allied Breweries – but only the 'big four' send their cider nationwide.

CIDER FAVOURITES FROM THE 'BIG FOUR'

Boardroom Special   *serves 12*
From Bertram Bulmer.

2 bottles dry Pomagne	2 wine glasses sherry
2 bottles dry white wine	2 wine glasses brandy
thinly cut lemon peel (with	6oz (175g) raspberries
absolutely no pith)	2 bananas, thinly sliced

Chill the Pomagne and wine, and place the lemon in a very large jug with the sherry 30 minutes before use. Mix all the ingredients well together and serve really cold.

Red Bullet
From Ian Howie, Merrydown.

One part gin or vodka	3–4 parts Merrydown Vintage
2 parts red currant wine	Dry Cider
lemon juice and peel	

Mix all the ingredients together and serve chilled. Start the party with three to four parts of cider and lengthen to eight parts as things begin to swing!

28

Fish and Cider Pâté   *serves 4–6*
From A. S. Hooper, Chairman, Taunton Cider Co.

1lb (450g) cod fillet	1 tbsp chopped parsley
6fl oz (175ml) Special Vat Cider	1 clove garlic (crushed)
4oz (100g) tomato purée	Worcestershire sauce
2 tbsp mayonnaise	salt and freshly ground black
1 tbsp anchovy essence	pepper

Wash the fish and place in a frying pan. Pour over the cider and gently poach till cooked. Leave to cool in the liquid. When cool remove fish and flake it removing bones and skin. Pour the liquid into a bowl and add the tomato purée and mayonnaise. Mix together then add the anchovy essence, parsley, garlic and a few drops of Worcestershire sauce. Mix till smooth or blend in a liquidiser. Season and chill. Serve decorated with lemon slices and watercress with hot toast.

Sunset Sip   *serves 12*
From Francis Showering, Chairman, Coates Gaymers – for serving at a Horkey supper, when farmers, families and labourers gathered after harvest for a blow-out supper in the barn, of hot beef, vegetables and plum pudding.

1 flagon Gaymers Olde English	1 apple
Cyder	good pinch of cinnamon and
½pt (275ml) lemonade	nutmeg
2 oranges	

Peel and slice one orange and squeeze the juice from the second. Peel the apple, remove the core and slice thinly. Add everything except the lemonade to the cider and leave for 2 hours in the fridge. Add the lemonade and serve.

2
A TASTE OF CIDER

I have organised the following recipes in conventional meal order but in fact planning of menus this way is a literary convenience rather than a necessity. Since cider is essentially an informal drink and makes no demands upon its users, there is no reason to stick with convention. You could try a large hors d'oeuvre as the main meal, some of the cakes as puddings, and a mini fish dish could be a starter. Though we should never scorn the wisdom of culinary wizards, cooking relies on individual inspiration, helped enormously by the promise of cooks' perks!

The sophisticated use of cider as a cooking aid is a fairly new discovery. Although country women have always substituted it for ale or wine, depending on whatever they had to hand, its versatility and excellent taste is the product of twentieth-century manufacturing techniques.

Menu planning itself could be the subject of a book. In the Middle Ages all food was placed on the table at the same time, with starters – or side dishes – placed along one side. Everything was served on a trencher – a huge piece of black unleavened bread – and those who were still hungry at the end of the meal ate the bread as well, swilled down with a flagon of ale or cider. Hence the modern saying 'he is a good trencherman'.

The first real menu as we know it was originated by the Duke of Brunswick in 1541 during the reign of Henry VIII, when unbelievable quantities of food were eaten. Even as late as 1913 Mrs Beeton was recommending nine courses for an ordinary family dinner party!

Today we eat less and, despite the critics of junk synthetic food, we eat far better, for we understand more about nutritional needs for health. Take any traditional British fare or traditional British festival and cider seems literally a natural nutritious ingredient of both. From Bubble and Squeak (the cockney re-

30

hash of yesterday's green vegetables and mash) to fish and chips or cockles and mussels; at Punkie Night (October 29th) when turnip lanterns were originally made to light home cider-sodden husbands; or on Pinch Bum Day when country folk celebrated the escape of King Charles I by pinning an oak leaf to their jackets. Those who did not were pinched by the children in the appropriate place.

So hopefully the selection of food and traditional festivals will whet your appetite and provide the inspiration for a get together – after all any excuse is good for a party!

Mischief Night, November 4th

A time when licensed lawlessness prevailed and every kind of prank was practised by the young folk – such as hurling gates into ditches. Might not go down too well today!

SAUCES AND ACCESSORIES

Drusilla's Apple Chutney

5lb (2.25kg) English cooking apples	4pt (2.2L) Martlet Cider Vinegar
1½lb (675g) demerara sugar	2lb (900g) onions
1 tsp salt	2lb (900g) sultanas
1oz cloves	½ tsp each of ground ginger, cinnamon and mixed spice

Cut apples and onions into chunks and cook in the cider vinegar, retaining ½pt (275ml). Add sultanas, spices and sugar. Steadily boil retained cider vinegar for 5 minutes, adding cloves. Add this now partly reduced clove vinegar to the other ingredients. Cook steadily until deep brown in colour. Keep closed with well-fitting lid whilst cooking. Allow to cool thoroughly before potting.

French Dressing

1 tsp cider	1 tbsp lemon juice or cider vinegar
1 tbsp oil	
pinch of salt and pepper	

Whisk all ingredients together.

Sauce Normande
Originated by La Varenne, Ecole de Cuisine, Paris. Serve with meats, and vegetables like cauliflower, leeks, salsify, carrots and celery. Makes 1¼pt (1L) sauce.

7 tbsp butter	2 cups Merrydown Vintage Dry Cider
¼ cup flour	
pinch grated nutmeg	1 cup double cream
few drops lemon juice	salt and pepper
1 onion, thinly sliced	

Melt 1 tbsp butter in a pan, add onion, brown slightly over low heat. Add half the remaining butter, mix well. Add flour and stir until mixture foams. Whisk in cider and bring to boil. Add salt, pepper and nutmeg and simmer for 7–8 minutes or until the sauce lightly coats a spoon. Stir in cream, bring sauce almost back to the boil. Remove from heat and whisk in remaining butter, a knob at a time. Add a few drops of lemon juice and season to taste. Do not reheat the sauce or butter will separate.

Cheese and Cider Sauce

¾oz (20g) butter
¾oz (20g) plain flour
½pt (275ml) dry cider
3oz (75g) Cheddar cheese, grated

1 eating apple, peeled, cored and
  grated
salt and pepper

Melt butter in saucepan, add flour and cook for a few minutes, stirring. Remove from heat, gradually stir in the cider, add the cheese and stir till melted. Add the apple and seasoning, mix well and re-heat. Serve hot with grilled mackerel or herrings.

Cider Sauce

A delicious sauce to accompany your favourite barbecued kebabs (enough for one serving).

1 tbsp cornflour
1 tsp dry mustard
½pt (275ml) Woodpecker cider

¼pt (150ml) stock (preferably
  bacon stock)

Skewer your chosen kebab ingredients, allowing at least two kebabs per person, and brush with oil. Place on a hot barbecue, turning from time to time. Give them approximately 3 minutes on each side.

    To make the cider sauce, mix the cornflour and mustard together, and blend with a little of the stock. Gradually add the cider and the remainder of the stock. Bring slowly to the boil and cook for 2 minutes. This sauce can be served hot or cold.

    Place the kebabs on a bed of boiled rice and serve with a tossed green salad and the cider sauce.
Or try this variation from Mrs Beeton herself.

½pt (275ml) cider
¾pt (425ml) brown sauce
2 cloves

1 bay leaf
salt and pepper

Simmer the whole until reduced to the desired consistency, then pass through a fine strainer or tammy-cloth, re-heat, and serve as a substitute for champagne sauce with braised ham or duck.

A Dash of Cider

... soak haricot beans in cider overnight before baking them.
... baste meat with cider, butter and meat juices from the pan.
... add dry cider to mincemeat.
... use still cider in making pastry for apple pie.

HORS D'OEUVRES

Coquilles St Jacques au Cidre   *serves 6 as an appetiser*
(Scallops with Cider)   *or 4 as a main course*

Originated by La Varenne, Ecole de Cuisine, Paris. The Principal, Anne Willan, learned her cooking in the kitchen of her parent's Yorkshire home.

1¼lb (575g) scallops	2 tsp arrowroot or potato starch,
3 tbsp butter	dissolved in 1–2 tbsp water
3 shallots, chopped	juice of ½ lemon
2 cups Merrydown Vintage Dry	1 tbsp chopped parsley
Cider	salt and pepper
¼pt (150ml) double cream	

Wash and dry the scallops and cut each into 2–3 diagonal slices. Melt the butter in a shallow saucepan, add the shallots and cook over a low heat for 2–3 minutes or until softened. Add the cider and salt and pepper. Bring just to the boil and poach for 1–2 minutes over a low heat. Remove the scallops and drain on paper towels. Boil the remaining liquid for 5 minutes or until reduced to 5 or 6 tablespoons. Add the cream, bring back to the boil, and gradually stir in dissolved arrowroot or potato starch until the sauce is thick enough to coat a spoon; season to taste. Just before serving return the scallops to the sauce and reheat gently. Add lemon juice to taste. Spoon into scallop shells or a shallow serving bowl, sprinkle with parsley and serve hot.

Smoked Kipper Pâté   *serves 6–8*
From the Craster Kipper Smokers of Alnwick, Northumberland.

8oz (225g) kippers	black pepper
4 tbsp Bulmers No. 7 (warmed)	4oz (100g) melted butter
2 tbsp cream or top of milk	

Remove skin from kipper and cut the flesh into small pieces. Put this along with all the other ingredients into a liquidiser. Blend until smooth. Serve in a small dish with lemon slices.

Shrimps in Cider   *serves 4*
From the Cider Museum, Valogne, Normandy.

1lb (450g) *live* prawns	25fl oz (750ml) cider
2pt (1.15ml) water	sea salt, pepper

Put the prawns in the liquid and boil for 5 minutes. Gut the prawns, adding seasoning to taste. Serve as an hors d'oeuvre or appetiser with thin buttered toast. The secret is in using live prawns!

Grapefruit and Orange Starters   *serves approximately 3*

1 grapefruit
2 oranges

6fl oz (168ml) Pomagne, chilled
glacé cherries

Peel the grapefruit and oranges, removing peel and pith. Cut segments of fruit carefully and mix together. Divide into glasses. Pour the chilled Pomagne over to just cover the fruit, and decorate with glacé cherries.

Mushroom Starter   *serves 4*

½lb (225g) small button
  mushrooms, sliced finely
¼pt (150ml) Merrydown Vintage
  Dry Cider
3 tbs oil
pinch each of dry mustard and
  chilli powder

2 triangular portions Camembert
  cheese
4 sticks celery
1 green pepper
8oz (225g) tin kidney beans
1 lettuce, shredded
1 tbsp chopped parsley

Marinate the sliced mushrooms in a mixture of cider, oil and spices for several hours in the fridge (or leave overnight if wished).

When ready to serve, finely slice or dice the cheese, celery and pepper. Strain the mushrooms (retaining the marinade) and mix well with the diced vegetables, cheese and drained beans. Place crisp shredded lettuce in four individual dishes and pile the mushroom mixture on top. Moisten each with 1 tsp cider/oil marinade and sprinkle generously with chopped parsley.

Salmon Mousse   *serves 4*

1 tbsp water
½oz (15g) gelatine
8oz (225g) tin red salmon
2 large eggs, separated
¼pt (150ml) single cream

¼pt (150ml) Gaymers Norfolk
  Dry Cider
½ tsp paprika
½ tsp salt
1 tbsp lemon juice

Put the water into a bowl and sprinkle on the gelatine. Place the bowl over a pan of boiling water and stir the mixture until the gelatine is thoroughly dissolved. Allow the liquid to cool to lukewarm. Flake the salmon. Beat the egg yolks into the cream. Combine the cider and the egg and cream mixture with the dissolved gelatine, and stir in the flaked salmon, paprika, salt and lemon juice. Beat the egg whites until stiff then carefully fold in the salmon mixture. Spoon the mixture into a round mould and leave to set in the refrigerator. When set firm, turn out the mousse from its mould and serve with sliced cucumber and tomato.

Grapefruit with Ginger
serves 4

2 grapefruit
dry cider
4oz (100g) demerara sugar

1½oz (35–40g) crystallised or stem ginger, roughly chopped

Cut the fruit in half, and cut off all the pith and membrane. Discard membrane, centre core and pips, and reserve the shells. Make the juice up to ½pt (275ml) with dry cider and pour into a saucepan. Stir in the demerara sugar and allow to dissolve over a low heat. Boil rapidly for 5 minutes. Mix the grapefruit flesh with the ginger and return to the grapefruit shells. Pour on the warm syrup and serve.

Creamy Avocados
serves 4

4oz (100g) cream cheese
¼pt (150ml) dry cider
2 sticks celery, washed and finely chopped

freshly ground black pepper
2 avocados, cut in half lengthways, stones removed

Reduce the cider to 3 tbsps by rapid boiling. Beat the cream cheese and reduced cider together until light and fluffy. Blend in the celery and black pepper. Divide the cheese mixture between the avocado halves. Serve immediately.

Tomato and Prawn Soup
serves 4–6

1oz (25g) margarine
1 medium onion, finely chopped
1lb (450g) tomatoes, quartered
2oz (50g) long grain rice
2oz (50g) lentils
½pt (275ml) chicken stock (made with 2 stock cubes)

½ tsp mixed herbs
salt and freshly ground black pepper
2 tbsp tomato purée
½pt (275ml) Special Vat Cider
3fl oz (75ml) single cream
4oz (100g) peeled prawns

Melt margarine in a large saucepan, cook the chopped onion until transparent, and then add tomatoes, rice, lentils, stock, mixed herbs and seasoning. Bring to the boil, cover and reduce heat to simmering. Cook until the rice is tender. Rub soup through a sieve and pour back into a saucepan. Add tomato purée and cider and bring to the boil. Reduce heat and gradually stir in the cream. Five minutes before serving add the prawns, check seasoning and stir thoroughly.

Serve in soup bowls garnished with either chopped parsley or a small sprig of watercress.

Note: If a thicker soup is preferred, add a little cornflour mixed with water before adding the prawns, and heat thoroughly.

Onions in Cider   *serves 6*

2pt (1.15L) sweet cider
2lb (900g) pickling (or small)
  onions

lemon juice
4oz (100g) seedless raisins
4oz (100g) dark brown sugar

Reduce the sweet cider by boiling rapidly, to a quarter its original volume. Cover the onions with cold water and a squeeze of lemon juice and bring to the boil. Remove from the heat. Skin the onions and arrange in a buttered heatproof dish. Sprinkle the raisins over the top. Add the sugar to the sweet cider, pour over the onions and cook in a moderate oven at 180°C (350°F) Mark 4, for 15 minutes. Serve cold on individual plates.

Herrings in Cider   *serves 4*

4 herrings
salt and freshly ground black
  pepper
1 small onion, finely chopped

1 apple, finely chopped
1 level tbsp chopped parsley
½pt (275ml) dry cider (such as
  Strongbow)

Remove the bones from the herrings, clean and lay flat. (The fishmonger will always do this for you if asked.) Season the inside of the fish with salt and pepper. Mix the onion, apple and parsley together and spread over the herrings. Roll up.

Grease an ovenproof dish and lay the fish in it. Pour the cider around them and bake in the oven at 180°C (350°F) Mark 4, for about 40 minutes. Serve the herrings with cider spooned over them.

Seafood in Cider Sauce   *serves 4*

4 plaice fillets
¼pt (150ml) milk
1 bay leaf
salt and freshly ground black
  pepper
4oz (100g) peeled prawns
2oz (50g) butter
1oz (25g) flour

¼pt (150ml) Gaymers Norfolk
  Dry Cider
1 tbsp lemon juice
1 tbsp double cream
4½oz (125g) packet instant
  mashed potato (made to
  manufacturer's instructions)
1oz (25g) fresh breadcrumbs

Fold the plaice fillets into three, skin side inside. Place into a pan and pour over milk. Add the bay leaf, salt and pepper, cover and poach for about 10 minutes or until tender.

Remove the fish from the milk (which you retain) and arrange on individual ovenproof dishes or one large one. Sprinkle the prawns over the fish. If necessary make up the poaching milk with more milk to ¼pt (150ml).

Melt 1oz (25g) of the butter in a small pan, add the flour, and gradually stir in the flavoured poaching milk, plus the cider. Bring to the boil, stirring all the time, and continue boiling, stirring until thick, smooth and glossy. Remove from heat and stir in the lemon juice and cream. Season to taste and pour over fish. Pipe a border of potato around, sprinkle with breadcrumbs, dot with the remaining butter, and brown under a hot grill.

Mayonnaise

2 eggs
1 level tsp French mustard
salt and freshly ground black
  pepper

good pinch caster sugar
1 tbsp Martlet cider vinegar
½pt (275ml) olive oil

Put the eggs in a blender goblet with the mustard, salt and pepper, caster sugar and cider vinegar. Switch on for 1 second. Add the oil very slowly at first and then in a steady stream with blender at top speed. When mixture thickens (the sound changes) add the rest of the oil.

For a change add a chopped dessert apple, cored, but with the peel still on.

Garland Day, May 1st

The Celtic calendar made May 1st the first day of summer, with Maypole dancing and parades of floral garlands ... and perhaps a Somerset Casserole for supper?

FISH

Somerset Casserole
serves 6–8

2lb (900g) filleted cod or haddock
salt and freshly ground black
  pepper
4oz (100g) mushrooms, sliced
5oz (150g) tomatoes, skinned
  and sliced

½pt (275ml) cider
2½oz (60–65g) butter
1½oz (35–40g) flour
1lb (450g) creamed potatoes
2oz (50g) Cheddar cheese, grated

Cut the fish into small cubes and place in a shallow, greased fireproof dish; sprinkle with salt and pepper. Add the mushrooms, 4oz (100g) of the tomatoes, and cider and dot with 1oz (25g) of the butter. Cover the dish and bake for 25 minutes in the oven at 200°C (400°F) Mark 6. Carefully strain off the cooking liquid, melt the remaining butter, stir in the flour and gradually add the liquid. Bring this sauce to the boil and cook for a few minutes. Pour the sauce over the fish, and pipe a border of creamed potatoes along the inner edge of the dish. Sprinkle with grated cheese and garnish with the remaining slices of tomato. Brown in a hot oven at 230°C (450°F) Mark 8, until the cheese is bubbling. Garnish with parsley and serve. This is a substantial lunch or supper dish.

Halibut in Cider
serves 8

From the English Tourist Board's *Taste of England Manual.*

8 halibut cutlets (6oz or 175g
  each)
salt and freshly ground black
  pepper
2 lemons
½lb (225g) onions, chopped
2 tbsp oil

1 clove garlic, crushed
1pt (550ml) dry cider
1lb (450g) tomatoes, skinned and
  sliced
1 heaped tbsp finely chopped
  parsley

Place the halibut cutlets in a greased fireproof dish, and sprinkle with salt, pepper and the juice of 1 lemon. Cook the onions gently in the oil for 5 minutes, add the crushed garlic, and cook for a few minutes more. Remove from the heat, stir in the cider and pour over the fish. Arrange the tomatoes on top and sprinkle with chopped parsley. Cover with buttered greaseproof paper or foil and bake in the oven for 20–30 minutes at 180°C (350°F) Mark 4. Serve with lemon slices and buttered new potatoes.

Mackerel with Gooseberry Sauce   *serves 4*

¾lb (350g) gooseberries
¼pt (150ml) sweet cider (such as
  Woodpecker)
1 rounded tbsp cornflour
1 tbsp cold water
1 tbsp sugar (or to taste)

4 small or 2 large mackerel,
  filleted
seasoned flour
2oz (50g) butter
juice of ½ lemon
1oz (25g) chopped parsley

Wash the gooseberries, place in a pan with the cider, and stew gently until tender, then sieve. Put the cornflour and the water in the saucepan and blend, stir in the gooseberry purée and return to the heat. Bring to the boil, stirring continuously and allow to thicken. Simmer for 2–3 minutes before adding the sugar, still stirring.

Dip the mackerel fillets in the seasoned flour. Melt the butter in a frying pan and fry the fish for about 6–8 minutes, turning once. Place on a warm serving dish. Add the lemon juice and parsley to the pan and heat through. Pour over the fish and serve with the gooseberry sauce.

Saturday Fish Pie   *serves 4*

1 14oz (400g) packet cod steaks
¼pt (150ml) medium dry cider
  (such as Dry Woodpecker)
milk
1½oz (35–40g) butter
1½oz (35–40g) flour
2 hard-boiled eggs, chopped

1 level tbsp chopped parsley
1 level tbsp chopped chives
salt and freshly ground black
  pepper
1lb (450g) potatoes, cooked and
  mashed with milk and butter
1oz (25g) Cheddar cheese, grated

Place the cod steaks in a pan and pour over the cider, cover and poach gently until cooked (about 15–20 minutes). Drain the cider into a measure and make up to ½pt (275ml) with milk. Flake the fish and put on one side.

Melt the butter in a saucepan and stir in the flour. Cook for 2 minutes. Add the cider and milk mixture to the pan. Bring to the boil, stirring continuously. Cook for 2 more minutes. Add the flaked fish, eggs, parsley and chives, and mix well. Season to taste. Turn into a well-buttered 2pt (1¼L) ovenproof dish. Top with mashed potato and leave in a cool place until the next day.

Heat the oven to 190°C (375°F) Mark 5. Sprinkle the top of the pie with grated cheese and bake for 30–40 minutes until golden brown and hot through.

THE MAIN COURSE

Potato Casserole
serves 2

2lb (900g) potatoes
1 medium onion, peeled and
   chopped
½pt (275ml) Strongbow Cider

salt and freshly ground black
   pepper
4oz (100g) Cheddar cheese,
   grated

Peel the potatoes and cut into thin slices. In a large ovenproof dish, arrange alternate layers of potatoes, onion and cheese (saving a little cheese to sprinkle on top). Season each layer, ending with potatoes on top. Pour in cider, cover, and cook for 45 minutes in the oven at 200°C (400°F) Mark 6 or until the potatoes are tender. Remove the lid, sprinkle with the reserved cheese and bake again until golden brown on top. Serve with bacon or ham, lamb, cold meats etc.

Cottage Surprise (Slimmer's Delight)
serves 2

1lb (450g) white cabbage
1 small cooking apple
1 tsp salt
1 tsp sugar (optional)
¼pt (150ml) Bulmers No. 7

4oz (100g) Red Leicester or
   Double Gloucester cheese,
   grated
parsley

Prepare the cabbage and shred. Peel the apple and slice. Put the cabbage and apple into a saucepan with salt and sugar. Pour the cider over the cabbage. Cook until quite soft but not 'soggy'. Place the cabbage into individual dishes or plates. Sprinkle with the grated cheese. Put under a hot grill until the cheese is golden brown, and serve garnished with parsley.

Viennese Stew
serves 4

1pt (570ml) Special Vat Cider
2 tbsp cider vinegar
2 small bay leaves
2 cloves
1 level tsp dried thyme
1½lb (675g) chuck steak, cut into
   1½in (3.75cm) cubes

1 large carrot, diced
1 onion, chopped
2 tbsp oil
2–3 level tbsp cornflour
salt and freshly ground black
   pepper
¼pt (150ml) soured cream

Place the cider, vinegar, bay leaves, cloves and thyme into a saucepan. Bring to the boil and simmer for 15 minutes. Cool.

Long Rope Day, Good Friday

When the seriousness of the religious festival was offset by the jollity of group skipping – exactly why, is not certain. But a good nourishing stew is filling fare for any energetic event!

Pour over the cubed steak and leave to stand overnight.

Remove the bay leaves and cloves from the marinade. Lightly fry the onion and carrot in the oil until tender, then fry the meat until brown. Pour the marinade over the meat, bring to the boil and simmer over a low heat for 40 minutes. Blend the cornflour with a little water until smooth. Pour into the pan. Bring to the boil, stirring. Season to taste. Remove from the heat and stir in soured cream before serving.

Taunton Vegetable Hotpot   *serves 4*

1½oz (35–40g) butter
1 large onion, sliced
1 large leek, trimmed, washed
   and sliced
8oz (225g) carrots, peeled and
   sliced
8oz (225g) swede, peeled and cut
   into 1in (2.5cm) cubes
8oz (225g) turnip, peeled and cut
   into 1in (2.5cm) cubes

1½oz (35–40g) flour
¾pt (425ml) dry cider
2 tsp Worcestershire sauce
1 level tbsp tomato ketchup
salt and freshly ground black
   pepper
1 chicken stock cube
1lb (450g) potatoes, peeled and
   sliced
3oz (75g) Cheddar cheese, grated

Melt the butter in a large saucepan and fry the onion, leek, carrots, swede and turnip for 10 minutes. Drain well, reserving the butter in the pan, and transfer to an ovenproof casserole dish. Add the flour to the saucepan and cook for 1 minute, stirring. Remove from the heat and gradually stir in the dry cider. Return to the heat and bring to the boil, stirring. Cook for a minute then add the Worcestershire sauce, tomato ketchup, seasoning and crumbled stock cube. Cook, gently stirring, for 5 minutes, then pour the sauce into the casserole. Arrange the potato slices on top. Cover and cook in the oven at 180°C (350°F) Mark 4 for 1½–2 hours, or until the vegetables are tender. Remove the casserole from the oven and increase the temperature to 200°C (400°F) Mark 6. Sprinkle the cheese over the potatoes and return the casserole, uncovered, to the oven. Cook for a further 15–20 minutes, until the cheese has melted and is golden brown.

Boiled Beef and Carrots   *serves 4–6*
From Harry H. Corbett, *Steptoe and Son*:

'I don't cook anything if I can help – but bung a bit of cider instead of water in anything and it tastes better. So how about this for a poshed-up version of a good old London standby. Loverly.'

3lb (1.35kg) brisket of beef (boned weight)
1 medium onion
cloves
1 bouquet garni
5 peppercorns
3 small bay leaves
salt and freshly ground black pepper

1¼pt (750ml) dry cider
water
3 large carrots, cut into ½in (1.25cm) slices
3 sticks celery, washed and chopped
1 tbsp horseradish relish
2 level tbsp cornflour

Roll up and tie the brisket with string. Soak in water for 30 minutes. Drain. Place the meat in a large saucepan with the onion studded with cloves, the bouquet garni, peppercorns, bay leaves and seasoning. Pour on the dry cider, leaving ½pt (275ml). Add enough water to just cover the meat, and simmer for 2 hours. Add vegetables 30 minutes before the end.

Lift out the meat, strain the liquid, then put the meat and vegetables on a dish and keep warm.

Measure ½pt (275ml) of the cooking liquid into a small pan. Stir in the horseradish relish. Blend the ½pt (275ml) dry cider and cornflour together, then stir into the pan. Bring to the boil, stirring. Cook for 1 minute. Pour over the meat and vegetables or serve separately.

Lamb Boulangère   *serves 6–8*

3½lb (1.6kg) shoulder of lamb, boned
½lb (225g) pork sausagemeat
1 rounded tbsp freshly chopped parsley
grated rind and juice of ½ lemon

salt and freshly ground black pepper
1½lb (675g) potatoes
½lb (225g) onions
½pt (275ml) dry cider (such as Strongbow)

Heat the oven to 180°C (350°F) Mark 4. Trim any excess fat from the lamb. Mix the sausagemeat, parsley, seasoning and the rind and juice of the lemon and spread over the lamb. Roll up and tie securely. Peel the potatoes and cut into thick slices. Peel and slice the onions and mix with the potatoes, then lay them in an ovenproof dish and season well. Put the lamb on top and pour over the cider. Cover with a piece of foil and bake for 30 minutes to the lb (450g) and 30 minutes over. After the first hour remove

46

the foil and baste the meat and potatoes before covering again. When cooked, sprinkle the potatoes and onions with a little further chopped parsley. Serve straight from the oven.

Lamb with Garlic and Lemon

serves 4

1½lb (675g) fillet of lamb, cut into strips
1 onion, sliced
1 small clove garlic, crushed
grated rind of ½ lemon
1 tbsp cornflour (optional)

½pt (275ml) strong medium dry cider
salt and freshly ground black pepper
freshly chopped parsley

Cook the lamb in a frying pan over a very low heat until the fat begins to run. Add the onion and continue cooking for a further 20 minutes, adding extra fat, if necessary, and stirring occasionally. Add the garlic, lemon rind and dry cider, bring to the boil, and simmer gently for 20 minutes. Add seasoning. If using cornflour blend with a little water first, then stir into the pan. Bring to the boil, and cook for 1 minute. Alternatively, transfer the meat to a serving dish and keep warm. Boil the sauce rapidly until it has reduced by half, then pour the unthickened sauce over the meat. Sprinkle with chopped parsley.

Spring Lamb en Croûte

serves 6–8

4lb (1.8kg) leg of lamb, boned
½pt (275ml) Woodpecker cider
1lb (450g) pork sausagemeat
¼lb (100g) bacon, rinded and chopped
salt and freshly ground black pepper
1oz (25g) butter
½lb (225g) onions, sliced

sprig of fresh thyme (or a little dried)
1 bay leaf
1 clove garlic, crushed
½pt (275ml) stock (from bones)
1lb (450g) bought puff pastry
1 large egg, beaten
1½–2 tbsp cornflour

Marinate the lamb in the cider for 2–3 hours, turning occasionally. Mix the sausagemeat, bacon and seasonings together. Take the meat out of the cider and dry on kitchen paper. Stuff the bone cavity with the stuffing. Sew up both ends with fine string.

Melt the butter in a large frying pan and brown the meat on both sides. Transfer to a casserole with the onions, herbs, garlic, marinade and stock. Cover and cook in the oven for 2 hours at 160°C (325°F) Mark 3. Remove meat from casserole and cool quickly. Reserve the juices.

Roll out pastry to an oblong approximately 20 × 10in (50 × 25cm). Brush the meat surface with beaten egg and dust with flour. Place the meat in the middle of the pastry and seal into a parcel. Trim off excess pastry and brush the parcel with beaten egg. Place the croûte, join side down, on a baking sheet. Make leaves for decoration with the trimmings. Bake in a hot oven at 230°C (450°F) Mark 8 for about 40 minutes.

Meanwhile, to make the sauce, remove excess fat from the braising juices. Mix a little of this stock with the cornflour in a cup, then pour back into the pan. Cook gently until hot and thickened.

Serve the meat on an oval plate, garnished with watercress, with fresh new potatoes, peas, and the sauce handed separately.

Lamb Shashlik
serves 4–5

From Northumberland WI.

1½lb (675g) lean lamb (from leg or shoulder)
1 onion, thinly sliced
¾ tsp salt
pinch of pepper

juice of 1 lemon
2 tbsp wine or dry cider
6 small tomatoes
6 mushrooms
butter or good dripping

Cut the meat into ½in (1.25cm) cubes, trimming off the fat. Place in a bowl with the sliced onion, seasoning, lemon juice and wine or cider. Mix well together and leave to stand overnight. When ready to cook arrange the meat on skewers, alternating pieces of meat with a whole tomato or a mushroom. Brush with melted butter or dripping and grill for 15 minutes, turning frequently. Serve the kebabs on a bed of savoury rice.

Lamb and Vegetable Curry
serves 2–3

1 onion, peeled and chopped
2 tbsp oil
1lb (450g) lean lamb, cut into cubes
1–2 cloves garlic, crushed
1–2 tbsp curry powder
½pt (275ml) cider

¼ tsp chilli powder (optional)
1 tsp tomato purée
salt and pepper
1 large potato, peeled and diced
a few cauliflower florets
1 tbsp each of peas, beans or other vegetables

48

Fry the onion in the oil, and then remove to a casserole. Fry the meat until brown, and put in the casserole. Fry the garlic, curry and chilli powders, and add the cider gently. Mix well, then stir in the tomato purée. Pour this over the meat in the casserole and season. Add the potato, cover, and put in the oven for 1 hour at 190°C (375°F) Mark 5. After the hour add the cauliflower and other vegetables. Return the covered casserole to the oven for a further 30 minutes. Garnish with onion rings before serving, with boiled rice.

The ideal drink to serve with a curry is an ice-cold bottle of dry cider.

Roast Leg of Lamb in Cider and Honey Sauce *serves 6–8*

1 leg or shank of lamb	¼pt (150ml) Gaymers Norfolk
salt	Dry Cider
2 tbsp honey	small sprigs of rosemary
1oz (25g) butter	

Wipe the meat, put into roasting tin, and rub the skin with a little salt. Put the honey, cider and butter into a pan. Bring to the boil and simmer until the mixture thickens. Brush over the meat. Using a sharp pointed knife make small incisions in the meat at about 2in (5cm) intervals, and insert a sprig of rosemary into each slit. Cover with foil and bake in a pre-heated oven at 180°C (350°F) Mark 4. Allow 25 minutes per lb (450g) plus 25 minutes. Baste from time to time.

Serve with vegetables in season with the juices poured over (which may be thickened if desired with a little cornflour).

Hereford Cider and Honey Gammon *serves 6–8*

3–4lb (1.35–1.8kg) gammon	½pt (275ml) Special Reserve
4oz (100g) brown breadcrumbs	Medium Sweet cider (plus a
2 tbsp brown sugar	little extra to bind the stuffing)
2 tbsp honey	

Cover the gammon with water and boil for 1 hour. Remove from water and peel away skin. Mix together breadcrumbs, sugar and the binding cider. Press this mixture onto sides of the gammon firmly, and place in a casserole or shallow dish. Pour in the ½pt (275ml) cider mixed with the honey. Bake for about 1¼ hours at 190°C (375°F) Mark 5, basting from time to time.

Pancake Day, Shrove Tuesday

The day when women race each other to the church tossing a pancake as they go. The prize? A kiss from the rector! Presumably the tossed pancakes are *un*-stuffed!

Savoury Pancake Fans   *serves 4*

4oz (100g) plain flour
½ level tsp salt
1 egg, beaten

½pt (275ml) dry cider
fat for frying

Filling

1oz (25g) butter
1 medium onion, finely chopped
2 sticks celery, chopped
1oz (25g) flour
½pt (275ml) dry cider
¼ level tsp mixed herbs
salt

10oz (275g) cooked turkey,
  roughly chopped (any cooked
  meat or poultry can be used)
6oz (175g) sweetcorn kernels,
  cooked
2 tbsp single cream (optional)

Sieve the flour into a basin with the salt. Make a well in the centre
and gradually whisk in the egg and dry cider. Use this batter to
make 8 pancakes in the usual way. Wrap the pancakes in foil and
keep warm while preparing the filling.

Melt the butter and gently fry the onion and celery. Stir in the
flour and cook for 1 minute. Remove from the heat and gradually
stir in the dry cider. Return to the heat, bring to the boil and cook
for 1 minute, stirring. Add the herbs, salt, turkey and sweetcorn.
Heat through and add the cream, if used.

Fold each pancake into four and stuff the fans with the turkey
filling.

Cidered Pork, Cheese and Apple Casserole   *serves 4*

From Mary and Roger Kingsley, The Refectory Restaurant,
Richmond, Surrey, who 'use a lot of cider'.

1½lb (675g) lean pork, cubed
½lb (225g) onions, sliced
oil or dripping
1oz (25g) flour
⅓pt (180ml) dry cider
a little grated nutmeg

salt and freshly ground black
  pepper
2 large cooking apples, peeled,
  cored and sliced
6oz (175g) Cheddar cheese,
  grated

Brown the pork quickly, together with the onions, in the oil or
dripping. Put the meat and onion in a casserole. Sprinkle flour
over juices left in the frying pan, stir, then gradually add cider
and seasonings. Cook until thickened, stirring, and pour over
meat and onion in casserole. Cover with sliced apple, then the
lid, and cook for 1 hour at 180°C (350°F) Mark 4. Remove the lid,

sprinkle on the grated cheese, and increase the oven temperature to 200°C (400°F) Mark 6, and cook uncovered for a further 30 minutes.

Ham and Pineapple   *serves 4*
From Denbighshire WI.

4 thick slices raw ham   about ¾pt (425ml) cider
4 slices of pineapple

Slightly grill the ham then place a slice of pineapple on each slice of ham. Place in shallow ovenproof dish in one layer and pour in the cider. Cover with lid or foil and cook in slow to moderate oven for 45 minutes.

Merrydown Chicken   *serves 6*

1¾pt (1L) cider vinegar   1 green pepper, seeded and sliced
1 large roasting chicken   2 tsp dried tarragon, or small
4 leeks, cleaned and sliced into   bunch fresh
   2in (5cm) pieces

Sauce
3oz (75g) butter   1 tbsp flour
½lb (225g) mushrooms, finely   5fl oz (150ml) single cream
   sliced

Bring the cider vinegar to the boil in a deep flameproof casserole, and add the chicken, leeks, pepper and tarragon. Cover the casserole and simmer very slowly for 1–1½ hours, turning the chicken over halfway through.

When cooked, carve and remove the chicken to a serving dish, and keep warm covered with foil in a very slow oven. Strain and reserve the vinegar stock, and add the vegetables to the chicken.

To make the sauce, melt the butter in a thick saucepan, add mushrooms and, when they are soft, stir in the flour. Slowly add the retained cider vinegar stock, stirring all the time over very low heat until the flour is cooked. Taste to see if a pinch of salt is required. Remove from stove, add the cream, and pour over the chicken.

Serve with rice and a garnish of watercress. In summer, substitute a large bunch of sliced spring onions for the leeks. Instead of rice, triangles of crispy fried bread may surround the chicken. This dish is equally good hot or cold.

King's Pyon Pork Chops

serves 6

6 pork chops
salt and freshly ground black
  pepper
8oz (225g) button mushrooms
2oz (50g) butter
1½oz (35–40g) flour
½pt (275ml) dry cider (such as
  Dry Reserve)

1 tsp fresh chopped herbs (or
  good pinch mixed dried herbs)
5fl oz (150ml) carton soured
  cream, or 5fl oz (150ml) carton
  double cream, soured with 1 tsp
  lemon juice
chopped parsley

Remove the rack from the grill pan and line the pan with a piece of foil. Lay the chops on this and season well with salt and pepper. Grill chops for about 15 minutes, turning once, or until they are crisp and brown. Transfer the chops to a serving dish and keep hot. Reserve the juices on the foil.

Fry the mushrooms gently in the butter for 2 minutes. Remove them from the pan. Stir the flour into the butter and cook, stirring, for 1 minute. Gradually add the cider, stirring constantly. Blend in reserved meat juices and herbs, and bring to the boil, stirring. Return the mushrooms to the sauce and simmer for 3–4 minutes, stirring constantly or until the sauce has thickened. Check seasoning. Add soured cream and heat gently. Do not allow to boil. Serve with the sauce poured over the chops. Scatter with fresh chopped parsley.

Norfolk Chicken 'n' Cheddar

serves 4

4 small chicken pieces
1 small onion, chopped
1 small clove garlic, crushed
1 tbsp oil
1 tbsp flour
2 tsp mustard powder
¼pt (150ml) chicken stock

½pt (275ml) Gaymers Norfolk
  Dry Cider
salt and freshly ground black
  pepper
3 tbsp single cream or top of milk
6oz (175g) Cheddar cheese,
  grated

Grill chicken portions until golden and tender. Remove and place in ovenproof dish. Fry onion and garlic in oil, then blend in flour and mustard. Cook for 1 minute. Remove from heat and add cider and stock slowly. Place back on heat and cook gently, stirring all the time, until thickened. Season, then add cream and half the grated cheese. Pour over the chicken in the casserole, sprinkle with the remaining grated cheese, and place in oven at

Gooding Day, St Thomas's Day, December 21st

To ensure a festive Christmas, old women went 'a-gooding', or begging, for gifts or money from shops and houses.

190–200°C (375–400°F) Mark 5–6. Bake for about 15 minutes, or until golden brown.

Merry Orchard Pheasant with Forcemeat Balls and Apple Cider Fritters
serves 4

Originated by Mrs Mary Hamlin, Abingdon, Oxon, winner of the second prize in the 1980 Merrydown/WI 'Taste of Cider' competition.

Brace small or 1 large young pheasant
8fl oz (200ml) Merrydown Vintage Dry Cider
3 tbsp Martlet Cider Vinegar
2oz (50g) flour

2 heaped tsp paprika
salt and freshly ground black pepper
3oz (75g) butter
2 tbsp cooking oil
2 tbsp honey

Sauce
¾pt (425ml) giblet stock (see method)

1 tbsp Calvados

Forcemeat Balls
2oz (50g) streaky bacon
2 eating apples
liver from pheasant
2oz (50g) walnuts, chopped
1 medium shallot, chopped
pinch each of nutmeg and cinnamon
grated rind of 1 lemon
1 egg, beaten

salt and freshly ground black pepper
2oz (50g) fresh white breadcrumbs
1oz (25g) breadcrumbs, lightly browned
2oz (50g) butter
2 tsp oil

Apple Cider Fritters
8 apple rings (see method)
juice of 1 lemon
2oz (50g) strong plain flour
1 level tsp paprika
2 tsp honey

salt and freshly ground black pepper
4 tbsp Merrydown Vintage Dry Cider
2–3fl oz (50–75ml) cooking oil

Ensure pheasants are young and tender. Hang them for about a week, then pluck, draw and truss, reserving the giblets. To make the giblet stock for the sauce, simmer the chopped giblets (except the liver) in about 1pt (550ml) water along with a chopped small onion and carrot.

Mix together the cider and cider vinegar and marinate the pheasant in this for 2 hours or more, turning several times. Drain well, and reserve the liquid. Mix together the flour, paprika, salt and pepper, and coat the bird or birds with this, reserving any remaining flour to thicken the sauce (see below).

Heat the butter and cooking oil in a pan and fry the pheasant gently all over until lightly browned. Transfer to a roasting tin. To the fat remaining in the pan, add the honey and the marinade liquid, and bring to the boil. Pour over the birds and place tin in a pre-heated oven at 190°C (375°F) Mark 5. Cook for about 1 hour, basting frequently (with the forcemeat balls in a separate tin alongside for the last 35 minutes or so), when the birds should be thoroughly cooked and nicely glazed, and the liquid reduced to a syrupy consistency. (If the liquid is too far reduced before the pheasants are cooked, add a little more cider.)

To make the forcemeat balls, remove rind and bones from the bacon and cores from the apples (*not* the peel). Cut the apples carefully into rings – 4 from each apple – leaving enough apple flesh to make 3oz (75g), chopped, for the forcemeat balls. (The rings are for the apple fritters, see below.)

Pass the liver, bacon, apple, walnuts and shallot through a coarse mincer, add spices, lemon rind, seasoning and fresh breadcrumbs, and bind all together with a little of the beaten egg. Form into about 12 small balls, roll in remaining egg and then the browned crumbs. Heat butter and oil in a small baking tin, and bake forcemeat balls for about 35 minutes alongside the pheasant, turning occasionally, until nicely browned. Drain on kitchen paper.

To make the apple cider fritters, marinate the apple rings in lemon juice. Mix together the flour, paprika, salt and pepper, add the honey, and then add the cider a little at a time until the batter is of a good coating consistency. This may be left to stand until just before the pheasants are ready. Remove apple rings from lemon juice, dry on kitchen paper. Coat with batter and shallow fry in the oil on both sides until golden and the apple *just* softened.

To make the sauce, add the flour mixture left over after coating the pheasants to the juices remaining in the roasting tin. Blend well together, then add the giblet stock and bring to the boil. Adjust seasoning and strain into gravy boat. Add the Calvados.

To serve, arrange the pheasants in the centre of a large oval dish, with forcemeat balls at either end and the apple fritters down each side. Garnish with watercress, and hand the sauce separately. Accompany with button sprouts (about ¾lb or 350g after preparing), julienne carrots garnished with a little chopped parsley (about ¾lb or 350g after preparing) and boiled potatoes dusted lightly with paprika (about 1½lb or 675g after preparing).

Rabbit Country Style serves 4
Originated by Mrs Joyce Brown of Wakefield, Yorkshire, winner of the third prize in the 1980 Merrydown/WI 'Taste of Cider' competition.

1 rabbit, jointed	12 button onions
3oz (75g) flour	2 sticks celery
salt and freshly ground black	2 red eating apples
pepper	Merrydown Vintage Dry Cider
2oz (50g) butter	

Forcemeat Balls

4oz (100g) white breadcrumbs	1 tsp dried thyme or 2 tsp fresh
1 egg, beaten	grated rind of 1 lemon

Coat the rabbit joints with seasoned flour, then fry in the butter until brown. Place in shallow ovenproof casserole dish. Prepare onions and cut celery into 1in (2.5cm) pieces. Place in casserole.

To make the forcemeat balls, mix the ingredients all together and form into walnut-sized balls. Place in casserole. Wash and slice the apples, leaving on peel. Place around the rabbit joints. Add salt and pepper, then pour over enough cider to cover the rabbit. Put on lid, place in oven set at 200°C (400°F) Mark 6, and cook until rabbit joints are done. Garnish with parsley. Serve with creamed potatoes, white cabbage and Brussels sprouts.

Merrydown Dilly-Dilly serves 4

1 duck (approximately 4½lb or 2 kg)	1 seedless orange, thinly sliced, with peel
salt and freshly ground black pepper	½pt (275ml) Merrydown Vintage Dry Cider
juice of 1 lemon and 1 orange	

Garnish

½lb (225g) grapes	parsley
granulated sugar	1 seedless orange, finely sliced
cider	

Hunting the Wren, Boxing Day, December 26th

A wren was killed and placed in the middle of a garland to be paraded round the town. Its feathers were later distributed for money as they were believed to be lucky.

Heat the oven to 170°C (340°F) Mark 3–4. Rinse the duck inside and out with cold water, dry well, then sprinkle inside and out with salt and pepper. Put the orange slices into the cavity. Place the duck breast-side up on a rack in a roasting tin.

In a small bowl mix together the cider and the lemon and orange juices and pour over the duck. Roast for 2 hours. Brush the duck with the hot cider mixture every 20 minutes and at the end of the cooking time use the liquid to make gravy.

To garnish, cut the grapes into small bunches, dip them into some spare cider, then into granulated sugar. Dry on a cake rack at kitchen temperature for about 1 hour.

Place the cooked duck on a warm serving dish and just before serving garnish with parsley, orange slices and frosted grapes.

Chicken with Orange and Cider
serves 4

1pt (550ml) dry cider	1 level tsp ground ginger
juice and finely grated rind of ½ orange	4 chicken portions
	1 level tbsp cornflour
1 tbsp soy sauce	fresh orange slices
1 tbsp clear honey	watercress

Place the cider in a saucepan, bring to the boil and boil rapidly until reduced to ½pt (275ml). Mix together the orange juice, rind, soy sauce, honey and ginger. Place the chicken portions in an ovenproof dish or roasting tin and brush the orange mixture thickly over the chicken. Cook uncovered in the oven at 190°C (375°F) Mark 5 for 20 minutes.

Remove from the oven, pour the reduced cider around the chicken and brush the remaining orange mixture over the portions. Cover the dish and return to the oven at 180°C (350°F) Mark 4 for a further 30–40 minutes or until the chicken is tender. Remove the chicken to a serving dish and keep warm. Blend the cornflour with a little cold water in a small saucepan and gradually stir in the cider juices from the pan. Bring to the boil, stirring constantly, and cook for 1 minute. Pour the sauce over the chicken portions and garnish with fresh orange slices and watercress.

Stir-up Sunday, November 22nd

The last Sunday before Advent when mixtures for Christmas puddings and pies should be stirred by each member of the family in turn.

DESSERTS

A First-rate Plum Pudding
serves 20+

From Lady Elizabeth Anson, director of Party Planners, who masterminds Royal and Society functions. Quantities could be halved.

8oz (225g) self-raising flour
1 level tsp mixed spice
½ level tsp grated nutmeg
1 level tsp salt
12oz (350g) currants
12oz (350g) sultanas
12oz (350g) stoned raisins
12oz (350g) fresh white
  breadcrumbs
12oz (350g) suet, finely chopped

4oz (100g) candied peel, finely
  chopped almonds
1 cooking apple, peeled, cored
  and grated
grated rind and juice of 1 orange
1lb (450g) soft brown sugar
6 eggs, beaten
¼pt (150ml) extra dry cider (such
  as Bulmers No. 7)

Grease two 2½pt (1.4L) pudding basins.

Sift together the flour, mixed spice, nutmeg and salt. Put the dried fruit into a bowl with the breadcrumbs, suet, peel, almonds, grated apple, orange rind and juice. Stir in the spiced flour and sugar. Finally add the eggs and cider. Stir the mixture well, then turn into the basins.

Cover the tops with greaseproof paper and a foil lid and let the puddings simmer gently in a large saucepan for about 7 hours. Top up with more water if needed. Lift them out of the pan, leaving the foil and greaseproof paper in place. Cool and store the puddings.

Simmer for a further 3 hours before serving.

Austrian Locksmith's Apprentice
serves 4

16 large prunes
16 blanched almonds
2oz (50g) flour
5 tbsp sweet cider (such as
  Woodpecker)

deep fat for frying
1oz (25g) grated chocolate
1oz (25g) caster sugar

Soak the prunes overnight. Carefully remove the stones from each prune and in its place put an almond. Place flour in a small bowl and stir in the cider; mix well to make a thick batter. Heat the fat for frying, coat each prune in the batter, and drop into the fat. Fry over a moderate heat for about 3 minutes until crisp and golden brown, then remove and drain on kitchen paper. Mix the chocolate and sugar together and roll the hot prunes in the mixture until each is lightly coated. Serve warm with whipped cream.

Rhubarb and Banana Surprise   *serves 4*

1lb (450g) rhubarb   5oz (150g) granulated sugar
4 small bananas   ¼pt (150ml) Autumn Gold Cider

Wash the rhubarb and cut into 1in (2.5cm) pieces. Place in an ovenproof dish with the bananas. Add the sugar. Pour the cider into a small saucepan and boil rapidly until reduced by half. Pour this over the rhubarb. Cover the dish and place in the bottom of the oven set at 180°C (350°F) Mark 4, for approximately 30 minutes until the rhubarb is soft but has not lost its shape.

Yorkshire Special   *serves 4*

6oz (175g) shortcrust pastry   4oz (100g) glacé cherries
2 handfuls raisins   3oz (75g) butter
¼pt (150ml) Merrydown Vintage   3oz (75g) caster sugar
  Dry Cider   2 egg yolks

Line an 8in (20cm) pie dish with the pastry. Put raisins and cider in a pan and heat gently until raisins swell. Cool, and drain raisins, reserving both raisins and cider. Cut cherries in half and line pastry base with these. Put butter and sugar in a pan, melt gently until sugar is dissolved, then boil. Mix cider with the egg yolks and add to butter and sugar in pan off the heat. Sprinkle swelled raisins over cherries and pour egg and cider mixture over and bake in oven set at 180°C (350°F) Mark 4 for 40 minutes until golden brown. Serve hot, or decorate when cold with whipped cream.

Mincemeat and Apple Tart   *serves 4–6*

1 large cooking apple   1lb (450g) shortcrust pastry
4fl oz (100ml) Autumn Gold   1lb (450g) mincemeat
  Cider   1 egg, beaten
granulated sugar

Peel, core, and thinly slice the apple and place in a saucepan with the cider and sugar to taste. Cook the apple to a purée and leave to get cold.

Line a shallow pie dish with about half the pastry (leaving enough for a lid and for decorations), and spread a layer of mincemeat over the pastry. When the apple purée is cold, spread on top of the mincemeat. Cover with remaining pastry, trim, and seal edges well. Brush the top with beaten egg. With any left-over pastry, roll out and cut out a Christmas tree to fit the top of the pastry. Place on top of the tart, brush with beaten egg, and place in the top of a pre-heated oven at 220°C (425°F) Mark 6 for 20–25 minutes or until golden brown.

Serve cold sprinkled with icing sugar, with whipped cream.

Upsidedown Surprise *serves 4–6*

2 large cooking apples
2oz (50g) caster sugar
9fl oz (250ml) Autumn Gold
   Cider
soft brown sugar

glacé cherries
4oz (100g) plain flour
2oz (50g) margarine
1oz (25g) icing sugar
1 egg yolk

Peel, core, and slice the cooking apples into a saucepan. Add the caster sugar and ¼pt (150ml) of the cider. Cook until the liquid has been reduced and the apples are puréed. Leave to cool. Reduce the remaining cider by half by rapid boiling.

Line the base of an 8in (20cm) tin with greased greaseproof paper and sprinkle liberally with soft brown sugar. Slice the glacé cherries in half and arrange, cut side uppermost, on the sugar. Spread the cooled apple purée over this. Rub together the flour and margarine, add the icing sugar and mix well. Stir in the egg yolk and enough of the reduced cider to make a stiff dough. Roll out and place on top of the apple purée. Place in the centre of oven at 180°C (350°F) Mark 4 for approximately 40 minutes until the top is crisp.

To serve, turn out on to a serving dish so that the fruit is on the top.

Note: Other fruit such as pears can be used instead of apples.

Strongbow Cheese Cake *serves 4*

4oz (100g) plain chocolate
   digestive biscuits
2oz (50g) butter, melted
½oz (15g) gelatine
¼pt (150ml) Strongbow cider

8oz (225g) cottage cheese
4oz (100g) cream cheese
1–2oz (25–50g) icing sugar
¼pt (150ml) double cream

63

Garnish
¼pt (150ml) double cream   fresh orange slices

Grease an 8in (20cm) spring clip or loose-bottomed cake tin. Crush biscuits and mix into melted butter. Press the mixture over the base of the tin. Dissolve the gelatine in the warmed cider, leave to cool but not to set. Sieve the cottage cheese and cream cheese, stir in the sugar and then add gelatine and cider mixture. Beat thoroughly. Whisk the cream until fairly thick and fold into the mixture. Pour over the base and leave to set.

To serve, pipe rosettes of whipped cream and arrange slices of fresh orange on top.

Meringue Surprise   *serves 4*

8fl oz (225ml) Autumn Gold   ¾lb (350g) soft fruit (raspberries
  Cider   or loganberries)
1 jam Swiss roll   caster sugar to taste

Meringue
4oz (100g) caster sugar   2 large egg whites

Reduce the cider by half by rapid boiling and leave to cool. Slice the Swiss roll into even-sized pieces and arrange in the bottom and around the sides of an ovenproof dish (glass if possible). Spoon the reduced cider over the Swiss roll. Wash the fruit, drain, and place on top of the Swiss roll. Sprinkle with a little caster sugar to taste.

To make the meringue, first keep aside 1 tbsp sugar (for the top of the meringue). Whisk the egg whites until stiff. Add ⅓ of the caster sugar and whisk again. Using a metal spoon fold in half the remaining sugar and then repeat the process. Gently spread the meringue over the Swiss roll and fruit, making sure it completely covers them, and shape into peaks.

Sprinkle the reserved 1 tbsp sugar over the top and bake in the centre of the oven at 150°C (300°F) Mark 3 until golden brown. Serve hot with pouring cream.

Gooseberry Delight   *serves 4*

6fl oz (175ml) Autumn Gold   6oz (175g) sugar
  Cider   2oz (50g) butter
1lb (450g) gooseberries, topped   4oz (100g) breadcrumbs
  and tailed   3 eggs

Reduce the cider to half by rapid boiling. Add the gooseberries and sugar and bring to the boil. Simmer until the fruit is soft and then put through a sieve. Pour the purée into a saucepan and add the butter. Gently heat to melt the butter. Place the breadcrumbs in a mixing bowl and pour over the purée. Stir well.

Beat the eggs and stir into the mixture. Pour into a greased ovenproof dish and bake in the centre of an oven set at 180°C (350°F) Mark 4 for approximately 1 hour, until the top has browned. Allow to cool a little before serving, with cream or ice cream.

Chocolate Apples and Pears

1 apple or pear per person	1oz (25g) sugar
½pt (275ml) Woodpecker cider	plain cooking chocolate

Choose well-shaped, firm fruit with a firm stalk. Leaving the stalk intact, peel the fruit thinly. Core carefully from the bottom (can leave whole if preferred). Put cider and sugar into a saucepan and gently heat. Add the fruit and poach gently for about 3 minutes. Do not allow the fruit to become too soft. Remove fruit and dry on kitchen paper. Allow to cool.

Place the broken-up chocolate in a basin and stand this in a saucepan of hot water. Simmer gently until the chocolate has melted. Coat the cold fruit with chocolate either by dipping the whole fruit in the chocolate or by holding the fruit over the bowl and spooning the chocolate over.

Serve in individual dishes or arrange on a large dish (a few of each look attractive). Serve with double cream or the reserved cider syrup.

A children's favourite is to serve these on sticks at parties or instead of toffee apples on Bonfire Night (best to leave cores in for this).

Handsome Maud's Special Trifle   *serves 6*

6 individual sponge cakes, split in half	3 egg yolks
raspberry jam	1oz (25g) caster sugar
8oz (225g) raspberries	1 heaped tsp cornflour
2oz (50g) ratafia biscuits	½pt (275ml) milk
8 tbsp Dry Reserve cider	¼pt (150ml) double cream
2 tbsp Calvados	½oz (15g) blanched almonds, split and lightly toasted

65

Sandwich the sponge cake halves together with the jam and arrange with the raspberries on the bottom of a shallow 2pt (1¼L) serving dish. Top with the ratafia biscuits and pour over the cider and Calvados.

Mix together the egg yolks, sugar and cornflour. Warm the milk in a saucepan over a low heat and pour it onto the egg mixture, stirring constantly. Return the mixture to the saucepan and cook gently, stirring until it thickens. Do not allow to boil or the custard will curdle. Allow to cool, then pour over the sponge cakes and leave to set. Whisk the cream until it is thick and spread it over the custard. Decorate with toasted almonds.

Blackberry Mousse   serves 4

8oz (225g) blackberries, fresh or frozen
4oz (100g) soft brown sugar
½oz (15g) gelatine

8fl oz (225ml) Merrydown Vintage Cider
5 fl oz (150ml) double cream
2 egg whites

Simmer the blackberries with the sugar in enough cider to cover. When soft, rub the fruit through a fine sieve, or liquidise and sieve to remove pips. Make up to ¾pt (350ml) with the cooking liquid, adding extra cider or water if required.

Soften gelatine in 2 tbsp water and dissolve in 1 extra tbsp boiling water. Add to the fruit purée and allow to cool and thicken. Whisk cream until thick, stir into the purée and mix well. Beat egg whites until dry and forming peaks. Fold into fruit mixture. Pour into a serving dish and decorate with cream rosettes, whole blackberries and angelica leaves, or as desired.

American Cider Sherbet   serves 12

1½lb (675g) apples, peeled, cored and sliced
6oz (175g) granulated sugar
1 tbsp lemon juice

½oz (15g) gelatine
3 tbsp cold water
½pt (275ml) sweet cider (such as Woodpecker)

Turn the freezer to its lowest setting.

Place the prepared apples in a pan with the sugar and lemon juice. Cover and cook slowly, stirring occasionally, until soft. Sieve or beat to form a smooth purée. Leave to cool. Place the gelatine in a small bowl or cup with the cold water and leave to stand for 3 minutes. Place the bowl or cup in a small pan of simmering water and leave until the gelatine is dissolved and clear. Cool slightly.

Mix together the gelatine, apple purée and cider, then turn into a rigid container and leave in the freezer until almost set. Turn into a large bowl and whisk until light and fluffy. Return to the container and freeze until solid. Remove from the freezer and leave to stand at room temperature for 10 minutes before serving.

Vintage Cider Jelly   *serves 6–8*

2oz (50g) gelatine
2½pt (1.4L) Merrydown Vintage
  Cider

2 breakfastcupfuls caster
  sugar

Soak gelatine in 3 tbsp cold water for 2 hours; then heat cider in a pan, and when it boils pour it onto the gelatine. Stir in caster sugar, mix well and strain into a mould. Allow to cool and set for 6–8 hours. Turn the jelly out onto a dish and serve, garnished with whipped cream, with sponge or macaroon biscuits.

Apricot and Cherry Sundaes   *serves approximately 6*
(depending on size of tall glasses)

1pt (550ml) Woodpecker cider
½lb (225g) dried apricots
1 tbsp cornflour or arrowroot
1oz (25g) caster sugar

1 tsp grated lemon rind
4oz (100g) cherries (fresh or
  tinned)

Soak the apricots overnight in the cider. If necessary simmer gently until soft. Blend cornflour or arrowroot (the latter gives a clearer juice) with a little of the cider, then stir in the apricots. Bring to the boil, and simmer for 1–2 minutes. Add sugar and lemon rind. Leave to cool. When cold arrange layers of apricot mixture and cherries in tall glasses. Chill. Decorate with whipped double cream and extra cherries.

Sparkling Fruity Jelly   *serves 4–5*

½oz (15g) gelatine
1pt (550ml) Cidona

fruit (mandarin oranges and
  grapes, for example)

Dissolve gelatine in a little of the Cidona by heating *gently.* Slowly stir this into the remaining Cidona. Add fruits of your choice. Put into individual glasses to set. Decorate with whipped double cream.

Cider Ice Cream with Cherry Sauce   *serves 4–6*

½pt (275ml) water
12oz (350g) granulated sugar
juice of 1 lemon

½pt (275ml) Dry Blackthorn
  Cider
½pt (275ml) double cream

Cherry Sauce
½pt (275ml) Special Vat Cider
½lb (225g) golden syrup

8 glacé cherries, finely chopped

To make the ice cream, put the water and sugar into a saucepan, and stir over the heat until the sugar is dissolved. Boil gently for 15 minutes. Cool. Mix together this syrup, the lemon juice and cider. Pour into a freezer tray and freeze. When half frozen, turn into a bowl, and stir in the whipped double cream. Return to the freezer tray and freeze.

  To make the sauce, reduce the cider to 5 tbsp by rapid boiling, then mix all the ingredients together in a small saucepan. Heat slowly until just warm.

  Serve the ice cream in individual dishes and spoon the cherry sauce over it.

Norton Fitzwarren Pear Delight   *serves 4*

½pt (275ml) Autumn Gold Cider
½in (1.25cm) stick cinnamon
2oz (50g) demerara sugar
4 ripe pears, peeled, quartered
  and cored

¼pt (150ml) double cream
½oz (15g) crystallised ginger,
  chopped
½oz (15g) shelled walnuts,
  chopped

Place the cider, cinnamon and sugar in a large saucepan or frying pan. Heat gently, stirring occasionally until the sugar has dissolved. Add the pears, bring to the boil, cover and simmer gently for about 10 minutes, or until the pears are just tender. Remove the pears from the cider and allow to cool.

  Rapidly bring the cider mixture to the boil and cook for about 5 minutes, or until syrupy. Allow to cool, and remove the cinnamon.

  Arrange the pears in 4 sundae glasses. Whisk the cream until stiff and use to decorate the pears. Sprinkle with ginger and walnuts and pour the cold cider syrup over the top. Chill slightly before serving.

Taunton Fruit Bowl
serves 4–6

¾lb (350g) gooseberries
¼lb (100g) blackcurrants
½lb (225g) strawberries

¼lb (100g) raspberries
¼pt (150ml) Autumn Gold Cider
6oz (175g) sugar

Top and tail the gooseberries and strip the blackcurrants from their stalks. Gently wash all the fruit and drain. Place the gooseberries and blackcurrants, cider and sugar into a saucepan and very gently bring to the boil. Reduce the heat and simmer gently until the fruit softens, but does not break. Leave to cool slightly and then pour into a serving bowl. When almost cold gently stir in the raspberries and strawberries. Place in the refrigerator to get cold. Serve with single or whipped cream.

Lifting Day, Easter Monday

The women of each house were lifted in a flower-decorated chair by the young men of the village. On Easter Tuesday it was the women's turn to lift the men – followed by Cider Cake and tea?

CAKES AND PASTRIES

Crunchy Cider Cake
serves 8–10

8oz (225g) self-raising flour
1 level tsp baking powder
3oz (75g) butter
3oz (75g) caster sugar

grated rind of 1 lemon
1 egg
¼pt (150ml) sweet cider (such as
  Woodpecker)

Topping
1oz (25g) self-raising flour
2oz (50g) soft brown sugar

1oz (25g) butter, melted

Heat the oven to 190°C (375°F) Mark 5. Grease and line the base of an 8in (20cm) loose-bottomed cake tin.

Sift together the flour and baking powder. Add the butter, cut into small pieces, and rub into the mixture. Stir in the sugar and lemon rind. Lightly beat the egg and add, with the cider, to the mixture, stirring well until blended. Turn into the cake tin.

Mix the flour and sugar for the topping in a basin; add the melted butter and stir with a fork until crumbly. Sprinkle over the cake. Bake for about 40 minutes until cake is risen and golden brown. Leave to cool in the tin for 5 minutes before turning out, then leave on a wire rack until cold.

Tuttifrutti Scones
makes approximately 12

¼pt (150ml) Special Vat Cider
2oz (50g) sultanas
2oz (50g) seedless raisins
2oz (50g) glacé cherries, chopped
8oz (225g) self-raising flour

pinch of salt
1½oz (35–40g) butter
approximately 3fl oz (75ml) milk
demerara sugar

Put the cider, sultanas, raisins and cherries into a saucepan. Bring to the boil and boil steadily until most of the cider is evaporated. Allow to become cold.

Sieve the flour and salt into a basin, and rub in the butter until the mixture resembles fine breadcrumbs. Stir in the fruit and cider and enough milk to mix to a firm consistency. Knead lightly. Roll out to ½in (1.25cm) thickness. Using a 2in (5cm) plain cutter, stamp out 12 scones. Place on a lightly floured baking tray and brush each scone with a little milk and sprinkle with demerara sugar. Bake at 220°C (425°F) Mark 7 for 10–15 minutes. Serve warm with butter.

Old English Cider Cake

1 tsp cinnamon
1 tsp baking powder
10oz (275g) plain flour
8oz (225g) butter
8oz (225g) granulated sugar
4 eggs

½pt (275ml) 'scrumpy' or dry
  cider
3 cooking apples, peeled, cored
  and sliced
sugar, to taste
1 eating apple

Blend the cinnamon and baking powder with the sifted flour. Cream the butter and sugar, then beat in the whole eggs, one at a time. Add a little of the flour mixture and a little cider to the egg and butter mixture alternately until everything is blended (using only half the cider). Pour the sponge mixture into a greased and floured sponge flan tin and bake in a moderate oven, at 180°C (350°F) Mark 4 for about 30 minutes, or until golden brown and firm to touch. Turn out and allow to cool.

Meanwhile purée the cooking apples with the rest of the cider and sugar to taste, and when cold place in the middle of the flan. Decorate with slices of eating apple just before serving.

Eccles Cakes
makes approximately 16

½pt (275ml) sweet cider
2oz (50g) mixed peel, chopped
4oz (100g) currants
¼ tsp mixed spice

2oz (50g) butter, softened
2oz (50g) soft brown sugar
1lb (450g) flaky pastry

Glaze
¼pt (150ml) sweet cider

2oz (50g) caster sugar

Reduce the ½pt (275ml) cider for the cakes to 2 tbsp by rapid boiling. Then put the peel, currants, mixed spice and reduced cider into a basin. Mix well together and leave to marinate overnight.

Cream together the butter and sugar and gradually work in the marinated dried fruit. Roll out the pastry thinly and cut into 3½in (8.75cm) rounds.

Place a spoonful of the fruit mixture in the centre of each pastry round. Draw the edges together to form a parcel and re-shape into a round. Turn the cakes over and roll lightly with a rolling pin until the fruit just shows through. Using a sharp knife, make 3 slashes on each cake. Place on a baking tray and bake at 220°C (425°F) Mark 7 for about 15 minutes.

To make the glaze, put the cider and sugar into a saucepan. Bring slowly to the boil, stirring. Boil until about 2 tbsp syrup are left. Brush the syrup immediately over the hot Eccles cakes.

Fruit Loaf

6oz (175g) sultanas
$\frac{1}{4}$pt (150ml) Woodpecker cider
8oz (225g) self-raising flour
4oz (100g) brown sugar

$\frac{1}{2}$ tsp cinnamon
pinch of salt
2oz (50g) butter

Topping
1 tbsp lemon curd

1–2oz (25–50g) sultanas

Soak sultanas in the cider for at least 2 hours. Put all dry ingredients into a bowl and add butter. Break up butter and mix in thoroughly. Add soaked sultanas and cider and mix well. Put mixture into a greased 1lb (450g) loaf tin. Bake in oven at 180°C (350°F) Mark 4 for about 45 minutes.

For the topping, warm the lemon curd gently in a saucepan and add sultanas. When the loaf is cooked, pour the melted curd mixture over it.

This loaf is best kept for a day or two before cutting. Serve as it is or buttered.

Almond Bars with Cider Glaze   *makes approximately 12*

8oz (225g) soft margarine
4oz (100g) caster sugar
2oz (50g) ground almonds
6oz (175g) self-raising flour

few drops almond essence
2oz (50g) sultanas
2oz (50g) flaked almonds

Glaze
$\frac{1}{4}$pt (150ml) sweet cider

2oz (50g) caster sugar

Put the margarine and sugar into a basin and cream together. Stir in the ground almonds, flour, essence and sultanas. Spread in a greased $11 \times 7 \times 1\frac{1}{2}$in ($27.5 \times 17.5 \times 3.75$cm) cake tin. Sprinkle the flaked almonds evenly over the top and press gently onto the mixture. Bake at 160°C (325°F) Mark 3 for 35 minutes.

To make the glaze, put the sweet cider and sugar into a saucepan and bring to the boil, stirring. Reduce by boiling rapidly until 2–3 tbsp syrup are left. Brush the syrup over the warm cake in the tin. Allow to become cold and then cut into small bars or squares.

Salter's Meadow Teabread

6oz (175g) currants
6oz (175g) sultanas
½pt (275ml) sweet cider (such as
  Woodpecker)

6 oz (175g) brown sugar
1 egg
12oz (350g) self-raising flour

Put the fruit, sugar and cider in a bowl and stir well. Cover and leave to stand overnight.

Heat the oven to 170°C (325°F) Mark 3. Grease and line an 8in (20cm) round cake tin.

Stir the egg and flour into the fruit mixture and mix thoroughly. Turn into the cake tin and bake in the oven for 1½ hours. Leave to cool on a wire rack and serve either sliced with butter or just as it is.

THE PICNIC BASKET

Summer Meat Loaf
serves 6

1 small onion
6oz (175g) pig's liver
8oz (225g) pork sausagemeat
8oz (225g) best minced beef
1 level tsp salt

½ level tsp pepper
1 rounded tbsp mixed fresh
  herbs, chopped
4 tbsp dry cider (such as Dry
  Reserve)

Garnish
1 tomato

chopped parsley

Heat the oven to 180°C (350°F) Mark 4.

Peel the onion, cut it in half and put through the mincer with the pig's liver. Place in a large bowl with the remaining ingredients and mix very thoroughly. Press the mixture firmly into a 1lb (450g) loaf tin. Stand the tin in a roasting tray of hot water in the centre of the oven and bake for 1½ hours. Leave to cool in the tin. Chill.

Turn out on to a serving dish and garnish with tomato slices and a thin line of chopped parsley down the centre. Serve sliced with a green salad.

Cider and Chicken Loaf
serves 12

1 3–4lb (1.4–1.8kg) chicken
4oz (100g) streaky bacon
1 onion, chopped
8oz (225g) pork sausagemeat
1 tsp mixed herbs

2 garlic cloves, crushed
black pepper
3fl oz (75ml) dry cider
2 bay leaves

Remove the flesh from the chicken and mince along with the bacon and onion. To the minced ingredients add the sausage-meat, herbs, garlic and pepper and mix thoroughly until smooth. Pour in the cider and mix again. Divide the mixture into two well-greased 1lb (450g) loaf tins or one 2lb (900g) loaf tin. Pat down well with the back of a spoon. Place the bay leaves on top, cover with tin foil and cook in a moderate oven at 190°C (375°F) Mark 5 for about 1 hour for the smaller tins, or 2 hours for the larger tin. When cooked allow to cool before turning out. Serve with a selection of fresh crisp salads, and crusty bread.

If you want to freeze the loaf, wrap it tightly in foil.

Cheese Rolling, Whit Monday

On Whit Monday at Brockworth in Gloucestershire young people race each other down the hill in pursuit of a rolling cheese. The prize is the cheese itself.

Prawn and Cheese Mousse
serves 10

½oz (15g) butter
½oz (15g) plain flour
½pt (275ml) sweet cider
8oz (225g) Cheddar cheese, grated
2 eggs, separated
2 level tbsp tomato ketchup

2 level tbsp chopped parsley
salt and freshly ground black pepper
8oz (225g) prawns, roughly chopped
½oz (15g) gelatine

Melt the butter, add the flour and cook for 1 minute. Remove from the heat and gradually stir in the sweet cider, reserving 3 tbsp for the gelatine. Return to the heat and bring to the boil, stirring. Cook for 1 minute and remove from the heat. Add the cheese, egg yolks, tomato ketchup, parsley and seasoning, and stir until the cheese has melted. Add the prawns.

Soak the gelatine in the 3 tbsp cider and then dissolve over a gentle heat. Cool, add to the cheese mixture, and mix in well. Whisk the egg whites until stiff and gently fold into the mixture using a metal spoon. Pour into a 2pt (1¼L) mould, and put in the refrigerator to set. Serve garnished with cress. Turn out at picnic site.

Cheese Aigrettes
serves 6

½pt (275ml) dry cider
2oz (50g) margarine
2½oz (60–65g) plain flour
pinch of salt

2 eggs, beaten
2oz (50g) Cheddar cheese, grated
deep fat for frying

Reduce the cider by half by rapid boiling, then place the cider and margarine in a saucepan and heat until the margarine melts. Boil, then remove from heat. Stir in the flour and salt. Return to the heat and stir vigorously for 1 minute. Cool. Gradually mix in the eggs and beat until mixture is smooth. Stir in the cheese. Fry teaspoonfuls of the mixture in hot fat for 5 minutes until golden brown. Drain, and serve warm with mixed salad.

Potted Cheese
serves 4–6

½pt (275ml) Special Vat Cider
¼lb (100g) butter, softened

½lb (225g) strong Cheddar cheese, grated

Reduce the cider to a quarter of its original volume by rapid boiling. Blend the butter and cheese together. Add the reduced cider and beat until smooth. Put into small earthenware dishes and place in the refrigerator to set. Serve with slices of toasted wholemeal bread.

Cheese 'n' Cider Loaf   *makes about 12 thin slices*

2oz (50g) butter   1 tsp salt
10oz (275g) self-raising flour   1 egg
4oz (100g) Cheddar cheese, $\frac{1}{4}$pt (150ml) Strongbow cider
  grated

Grease a 1lb (450g) loaf tin. Rub the butter into the flour and salt. Mix in the grated cheese. Add the egg and cider and mix until fairly smooth. Knead slightly then put into the loaf tin. Bake in a moderately hot oven at 190°C (375°F) Mark 5 for about 1 hour until golden brown. Serve hot or cold spread with butter. It is delicious served with soup or chunks of Cheddar cheese.

Meat Loaf   *serves 12*

1lb (450g) minced beef   salt and freshly ground black
1lb (450g) pork sausagemeat   pepper
1 medium onion, peeled and   1 large egg
  finely chopped   4 tbsp dry Woodpecker cider
1 tsp mixed herbs   4–6 rashers streaky bacon (to line
2oz (50g) breadcrumbs   tin)

Place all ingredients (apart from the bacon) into a mixing bowl, and mix thoroughly. Lightly grease a 2lb (900g) loaf tin or two 1lb (450g) tins. Line with streaky bacon.

Place the mixture into the tin or tins a little at a time, pressing down firmly. Cover with foil and bake in a moderate oven at 190°C (375°F) Mark 5 for 1 hour if using the smaller tins (for $1\frac{1}{2}$ hours if using the large tin).

When cooked turn out onto a serving plate. This loaf is delicious served hot or cold, in sandwiches, with salads, hot with vegetables, cold with chops, ideal for picnics. When cold, it slices easily and is very economical. It also freezes well.

3

MAKE YOUR OWN

Just as every pip in every apple produces a tree with a fruit flavour of its own, so home-brewed ciders can be as variable as the weather, which is why they are usually unreliable for cooking. But cidermaking is an adventure, an act of creation, and though each may have his own private ritual the drinking of the results is a pleasure to be shared!

Home cider production has always been an idiosyncratic business. There are books for purists which will tell you exactly how it should be done scientifically. There are books which tell you how to build your own press and your own mill from parts of a washing machine and car spares, and articles in magazines which claim that the blender on a liquidiser will do. A little browsing in the Spring is enjoyable but in the end you will go your own way as cidermakers have for centuries before.

So here are a few, simple, very different suggestions from country folk which will yield very different ciders – good sampling!

From Molly Harris (Martha Woodford) of 'The Archers'
The Archers, the BBC's best known and certainly longest lived farming family, have over the years been easing the pressures of workaday life for millions of listeners with a daily dose of gentle rural life. Old Walter Gabriel was a scrumpy drinker and now the Grundys make their own rough stuff in the barn. But real-life Molly Harris, who plays Postmistress Martha, has her own easy, economical way of using up windfalls.

Lightly rinse the apples in cold water, chop them up small and place in an earthenware crock or a plastic bin. Cover with cold water, cover with a cloth and leave to stand for 10 to 12 days during which time the contents will start to

79

The time-honoured method of pressing and milling

ferment. After 12 days strain the contents and add 1½lb (675g) sugar to each gallon (3.8L) of juice. At this point add a slice of beetroot to improve the colour and remove after a couple of hours. Now pour the cider into bottles, cork very lightly (don't use screw tops) and leave for two weeks. By then the working should have stopped. Cork securely. In three months you should have lovely sparkling cider.

From Mrs L. J. Whitlock of the West Kent Women's Institute
A very refreshing all-year-round drink which can be made from any apples. The yield is roughly equal to the amount of water used.

3lb (1.35kg) apples	1½lb (675g) sugar
6 quarts (5.7L) cold water	2 lemons

Cut apples as for making jelly (do not remove skin or core); put through a blender, or mincer. Cover pulp with the cold water. Allow to stand for a week stirring night and morning. Strain off liquid. Throw away pulp. Add grated rind and juice of 2 lemons and sugar to the liquid. Leave for 24 hours stirring occasionally.

Strain through muslin and bottle in screw-top bottles. If kept more than a week – open carefully.

From Hethersgill Women's Institute, Cumberland

2lb (900g) apples	$\frac{1}{2}$ tsp powdered cloves
2oz (50g) root ginger, well	cinnamon
bruised	1lb (450g) sugar

Rub the apples through a grater, or liquidise, and add 1 gallon (3.8L) of cold water, along with the ginger, cloves and cinnamon. Stir every day for a week. Strain and add 1lb (450g) sugar to the liquid. Stir until the sugar melts and bottle in screw-top bottles.

From Jo Deal, Founder of the Axe Vale Guild of Winemakers and author of *Making Cider* published by *Amateur Winemaker*. This is a rather more complex and scientific way of working which should produce correspondingly professional results! To make this sparkling dry cider, you will need to do some homework first. Makes 1 gallon (3.8L).

10lb (4.5kg) sharp apples	champagne yeast tablet
5lb (2.25kg) crab or bittersweet	1 tsp liquid petalose
apples	campden tablet
5lb (2.25kg) sweet apples	5 tsp granulated sugar

Extract juice – by blending, pressing or pulping – from the apples. Take out 4fl oz (100ml) and pour into small bottle adding crushed yeast tablet and 1 tsp sugar. Place bottle in a basin of hot water and when lukewarm remove and put into a warm airing cupboard for two days to start fermenting. Add the crushed campden tablet to the juice and leave for 48 hours. Test the specific gravity (with a hydrometer); if it is below 1,050 add sufficient sugar to raise the gravity of 1 gallon (3.8L) of juice by 5°. Add pectalose and fermenting yeast to the juice, pour into a gallon jar and fit an airlock filled with water. Keep in warm kitchen (60°F or 15°C). After two weeks when a sediment will have formed, rack into a specific fresh container and test specific gravity which should read 1,010 to 1,015. Siphon off into a fresh container fitted with an airlock and put into cool place for two weeks till specific gravity reaches 1,1005 (no less). The cider is now ready to bottle into beer or cider bottles topped up with 1 tsp of the sugar to each quart. Leave a 2in (5cm) gap at the top of each bottle. Fit proper metal snap closures.

Drinking vessels: (a) A costrel – the wooden barrel in which labourers took their cider to the fields. (b) An owl – for keeping cider cool. (c) A three-handled mug passed round from one to another – a kind of loving cup. (d) The Scudamore flute – the original, engraved crystal goblet, made for the Earl of Scudamore, is in the British Museum. (e) A cider 'straw' – made today by the potter-friars of Aylesford Priory, Kent

4

HERE'S HEALTH

I consider, and those I represent consider, that cider is a non intoxicating beverage. It is an exceedingly healthy beverage; it is of purely English and domestic manufacture and has various subtle actions on the internal economy that are better described in medical treatises than on the floor of the House.

> Mr Stanley Baldwin during the Finance Bill,
> October, 1909.

Champion of cider – at that time one of the most lucrative industries in the country – he may have been, but Mr Baldwin got his facts fuddled. For whatever its medical benefits cider *is* strong!

Many supermarket ciders today pack as powerful a punch as some wines and beers, yet parents still give it to children for parties as though it were a fizzy drink. So it's a good plan when shopping to know your way around the brand leaders. A medium-strength pub beer is about 4.5% alcohol by volume, and there are some varieties of cider that can be as much as three times as strong as a pint of beer.

Here is the alcohol content, by volume, of some better known ciders, and a check on their calorie content for weight watchers too!

	Alcohol %	Calories per ½pt or 300ml
Coates Triple Vintage	8.2	189
Pomagne Sweet (Bulmers)	8.0	187
Pomagne Dry (Bulmers)	8.0	151
Merrydown Vintage	7.5	179
Merrydown Vintage Dry	7.5	155

Taunton Exhibition	8.2	150
Gaymer's Olde English	6.0	126
Strongbow (Bulmers)	5.25	102
Dry Blackthorn (Taunton)	5.0	100
Special Vat (Taunton)	5.6	115
Merrydown Strong Still	5.8	150
Woodpecker (Bulmers)	3.5	80
Autumn Gold (Taunton)	3.2	100
Coates Somerset	4.0	90

ALLSORTS OF CIDER

Draught cider is cider from a cask or large container; it is never from a bottle.

Hard cider is the American term for ordinary cider. In the United States, 'cider' is unfermented apple juice.

Scrumpy is farm cider. It is still and dry (devoid of sugar), high in alcohol, usually cloudy and often vinegary.

Sparkling cider is fizzy. It contains carbon dioxide which may be added in one of two ways. The first method is to retain the fermentation gas, as in Champagne, although it is now illegal to apply this name to cider. The other method is to force gas into the drink when chilled, a process known as carbonation.

Still cider is not carbonated and is usually sold in half gallon or gallon jars.

Strong cider has a high alcohol content.

Vintage cider is made from the apple crop of any one year, rather than a blending of the pressings from several years' crops.

It will beggar a physician to live where all cider and perry are in general use.

Treatise of Fruit Trees, 1657.

The health benefits of cider, and especially cider vinegar which is made from it, have been proclaimed as a cure for everything from headlice to hypertension. For centuries they have been credited with mysterious powers akin to magic. Despite its rather rumbustious reputation amongst farmworkers and, in this century, amongst holidaymakers to West Country pubs where the rough stuff is available on draught, the best cider, drunk with caution, is a natural drink free from additives of any sort.

In 1664 the diarist John Evelyn wrote: 'Generally all strong and pleasant cider cleanses the stomach, strengthens digestions, and infallibly frees the kidneys and bladder from breeding the gravel stone.' Defoe and Francis Bacon also acclaimed it.

As early as 1630 it was believed cider was 'a drink both pleasant and healthy, much desired of seamen for long southern voyages'. Certainly Captain Cook took a supply with him to prevent scurvy on his second journey to the South Seas.

During the heyday of cider production, however, Devonshire colic was for years attributed to cider. It was often fatal. But in 1760 Dr George Baker, later President of the Royal College of Physicians, proved that it was caused by the lead linings in mills and presses, not by cider at all.

In the late nineteenth and early twentieth centuries, two eminent medical men, one in France and one in America, conducted clinical experiments with cider and cider vinegar as a medicine and produced, as a result, some learned papers which proved a godsend to cidermakers! Dr Edouard Denis-Dumont wrote *The Medical and Hygienic Properties of Cider and its Manufacture*, which attributed the fine robust health of the people of Normandy to their love of cider, and thirty years later Dr DeForest Clinton Jarvis, of the University of Vermont, wrote *Folk Medicine* which was to become a world best seller.

Folk Medicine is a small thought-provoking book based on Dr Jarvis's study of the ancient folk remedies of sturdy mountain villagers of Vermont. In it he says, 'I believe that the doctor of the future will be a teacher as well as a physician . . . Doctors will be even busier than they are because it is a lot harder to keep people well than it is to get them over a sickness.' Jarvis's theories are controversial and wide-sweeping and his claims for the uses of cider vinegar cover the treatment of arthritis, kidney trouble, obesity and headaches. His followers are unshakeable, and, certainly, his effect on the British cider vinegar business is undisputed! Today, with four main producers, it is a fully fledged industry in its own right supported by a host of health recipe books. To learn more about the uses of cider vinegar and its value to humans and animals you should contact the Vinegar Brewers' Federation, 186 City Road, London EC1V 2NU.

Barbara Cartland's Special Recipe for Sleep

When you find it difficult to sleep, mix a large teaspoonful of honey with a tablespoonful of cider vinegar – I prefer Aspall's which is organically grown – in a tumbler of water. Drink with four to five Dolomite tablets.

Also take one or two GEB 6 – the 'Stress Pill' – every day.

I promise you will sleep deeply and dreamlessly all through the night.

Headache Medicine

An old remedy for headaches.

1 quart (950ml) of cider	3 tbsp whole burdock seed
3 tbsp white mustard seed	1 horseradish root

Keep in a tightly corked bottle and take a wineglass full three times a day.

5

CIDER LORE

Wassailing was a pagan fertility rite which took place in the early New Year, usually on Twelfth Night. The roistering songs that were sung, long before carols were thought of, were aimed to bring good fortune and prolific crops. As apple farming became more important, so Apple Wassailing in the West Country and Howling in the South East developed a folklore of their own, and became an excuse for village merrymaking.

A gang of farmworkers led by the captain would go from orchard to orchard singing, shouting and pelting the trees with apples. Villagers prepared a huge pan of cider, sometimes with apples bobbing in the steaming brew, and in turn drank and poured cider over the roots of the oldest tree in each orchard. Often shots were fired, saucepan lids banged and there was much shouting.

The ceremony always had four symbolic elements: the ritual song and dance; a libation of cider poured over the tree roots to carry the lifejuice from one year to the next; the noise to awaken the life force and scare evil spirits; and the toast – a relic of sacrifice to Pomona, the Roman goddess of garden fruits.

These festivities were carried on without a break until this century when they died out except for a few places in the West Country. In 1906 the *West Sussex Gazette* reported that Mr Richard 'Spratty' Knight had led the Duncton Gang for fifty-four years.

Dressed in what some would describe as a grotesque costume principally composed of patches rivalling the rainbow in multitudinous tints, the whole surmounted by an indescribable hat, displayed in front a huge rosy cheeked apple, he heads a procession of villagers carrying horns and such lowly musical types as bits of gas piping.

Wassailing

Today, Morris Men perform the same rituals.

> Here stands a jolly good old apple tree
> Stand fast, root, bear well
> Every little bough
> Bear an apple now
> Every little twig bear an apple big
> Hats full, caps full
> Who whoop holloa
> Blow, blow the horns.

Hot Apple Punch   *makes 10 good glasses*

From the Taunton Cider Company who have recently revived wassailing in their own orchards at Norton Fitzwarren in Somerset.

2 × 25fl oz (700ml) bottles of Pommia, medium sweet	¾ tsp cinnamon
	4oz (100g) demerara sugar
3 tbsp Calvados	11 apples, cored and thinly sliced

Blend together and simmer for 15 minutes (do not boil).

Cider Mulled Punch   *serves 8*

2 small eating apples	¼pt (150ml) water
6 cloves	1 small orange
4in (10cm) cinnamon stick	1 bottle of sweet Woodpecker
2 level tsp ground ginger	cider
2oz (50g) soft brown sugar	

Remove the cores from the apples and a 1in (2.5cm) strip of peel from tops. Stick 2 cloves into the sides of each and bake in the oven at 180°C (350°F) Mark 4. Meanwhile put the remaining 2 cloves, the cinnamon stick broken into four pieces, ginger, sugar and water into a medium pan. Heat slowly till sugar dissolves and simmer for 5 minutes. Remove from heat, add orange cut into thin slices, and leave to stand. When the apples are cooked transfer them to punch bowl and cut the flesh without removing it from the skin. Strain spice water into punch bowl, pour in cider and serve at once.

Stuffed Jacket Potatoes

serves 4

4 large potatoes, scrubbed
oil
2oz (50g) bacon, diced
¼lb (100g) mushrooms, sliced

salt and black pepper
2fl oz (50ml) Special Vat Cider
2oz (50g) butter

Rub the skin of the potatoes lightly with oil, and bake in the oven at 220°C (425°F) Mark 7 until soft. Meanwhile, place bacon in pan and brown, then add mushrooms, seasoning and cider and cook until cider is absorbed.

Cut tops off potatoes when done, and scoop out pulp into a bowl. Add butter and mash well, then add bacon mixture. Mix together, spoon the stuffing back into the potatoes and return to a low oven at 160°C (325°F) Mark 3 for 10 minutes.

The Copper family have lived in and around Rottingdean, Sussex, since the late sixteenth century, working, until recently, on the land as shepherds and farmworkers. They still sing the traditional songs handed down from their ancestors. George Copper, born in Rottingdean in 1784, used to sing several of the songs and in 1897 his grandsons, James and Thomas, who had added to the family repertoire, were made honorary founder members of the English Folk Song Society on its formation. Through television and radio broadcasts and a number of recordings the songs are now widely known and sung at folk clubs all over the world.

Bob Copper, James's grandson, still remembers with delight the joy of 'sausengers' boiled in cider.

Every Sunday morning when I was a boy, and if there was an 'R' in the month, we had boiled pork sausages for breakfast bought from Mr Roberts, a small-holder from Chailey, who travelled down to Rottingdean on a Saturday in a horse and trap laden with farm produce – eggs, fruit, chickens, joints of pork to order and 'sausages in season'. The pork was coarse-cut, speckled with chopped sage and rosemary and well-peppered, with a touch of mace. My grandfather always called them 'sausengers', and this seemed to distinguish them from their pallid, insipid, town-bred counterparts. Boiling them brought out the delicious flavours of the herbs and spices and when boiled in cider they were nothing short of ambrosial. I don't recommend this treatment for what I call 'town sausages', but sausages worthy of the name 'sausengers' are still available at good butchers' shops if you search for them. I know several in East Sussex.

CIDER PLACES

For cider enthusiasts there are a growing number of places to visit where you can sample the local brew. Apart from the main manufacturers who, given advance warning, can generally arrange tours, there are now several small museums and cider centres.

Berkshire   The National Folk Museum at Reading has a display of cidermaking equipment.

Durham   Contact the Northumbria Tourist Board for details of the annual cider festival.

Hereford   The Cider Museum takes a cool, evocative dip into the past and looks at Bulmers' role in the story of cider. Attractions include a shop, tastings and a working cooper.

Normandy   The extensive, picturesque cider museum at Valognes tells the French side of the story.

Shropshire   Sheppys is a small cider museum where traditional farm cider is still produced. Based at Bradford-on-Tone, Sheppys is open from Easter to Christmas.

Suffolk   The Cyder House at Aspall near Debenham, Stowmarket, makes cider and cider vinegar from organically grown, non-sprayed fruit. The business has been in the same family for over 250 years.

Sussex   The Garden of England cider exhibition run by Merrydown is based at the Valley Wine Cellars (attached to Drusilla's Zoo) near Alfriston on the South Downs. It is open all year for booked tours, and a beer and cider festival is held there on the weekend before the August Bank Holiday.

Wales   The Welsh Folk Museum at St Fagans, Cardiff, has a display of cidermaking equipment.

CIDER TALK

A beetle   A sort of pestle

Cheese   The 'envelope' of cloth in which pummace is pressed

Chuter   The stone or wood base of the press on which the cheese is built

Codling   The moth which brings blight to apple trees

Costrel   A miniature barrel in which farmworkers carried cider to the fields

Hair   The cloth (formerly horsehair) which is used to make the cheese

Hedgehog   The spiked rotating drum on a rotary mill

Hogshead   A barrel containing approximately 50 galls (225L)

Keeving   A method of improving rough cider for social drinking by allowing it to stand, open-topped, in keeving vats before syphoning into casks with a bag of herbs

Lugg   The hook at the end of a panking pole

Mother   The jelly-like mass which appears in faulty cider

Owl   A round earthenware container in which the two handles form large 'eyes'

Panking Pole   The long pole with which apples were once knocked from the tree

Pipe   A barrel containing 120 gallons (540L)

Pomarium   An apple store

Pummace   The leftover pulp, after pressing, often used for cattle fodder

Purr   The weak first pressings, also known as ciderkin

Scratter   A rotary mill, rather like the Ingenio

Scrumpy   Rough cider made from scrumps, i.e. windfall apples

Truck   The payment of cider to labourers instead of cash, a practice which was banned in 1887

Tump   A pile of maturing apples

Wringehowse   The medieval word for a millhouse

INDEX

95